The SecRet Life of LANGUAGE

The SecRet Life of LANGUAGE

Discover the origins of global communication

SIMON PULLEYN

FIREFLY BOOKS

A FIREFLY BOOK

Published by Firefly Books Ltd. 2018

First printing

Publisher Cataloging-in-Publication Data (U.S.)

Library of Congress Control Number: 2018939508

Library and Archives Canada Cataloguing in Publication

Pulleyn, Simon, author
        The secret life of language : discover the origins of global
communication / Simon Pulleyn.
Includes index.
ISBN 978-0-228-10092-8 (softcover)
        1. Historical linguistics. 2. Language and languages.
I. Title.
P140.P85 2018   417'.7   C2018-901915-8

Published in the United States by
Firefly Books (U.S.) Inc.
P.O. Box 1338, Ellicott Station
Buffalo, New York 14205

Published in Canada by
Firefly Books Ltd.
50 Staples Avenue, Unit 1
Richmond Hill, Ontario L4B 0A7

Printed and bound in China

First published by Cassell,
a division of Octopus
Publishing Group Ltd
Carmelite House
50 Victoria Embankment
London EC4Y 0DZ

Contents

Introduction

The Holy Roman Emperor Charles V said that to possess another language is to possess another soul. The American linguist Charles Berlitz said that to speak only one language was like having a big house but living in only one room. Both had a point: languages go to the heart of who we are.

Something like 7,000 languages are spoken on Earth at the time of writing. They are not just 7,000 annoyingly varied ways of labelling the same thing; speakers of different languages really do interact differently with the world. If you speak a language with gendered nouns, like Italian, you see the inanimate world (for better or worse) as shot through with male and female associations. If you speak Russian and you want to say that you are going somewhere, you have to give information every time that most other European languages do

not require. You must first select a verb that shows whether you are going on foot or by transport; then you must indicate whether the travel is one-way or involves a return trip. Speakers of Japanese routinely have to think about an elaborate system of politeness and status rules when choosing which words to use for which addressee. In some Amazonian languages, if you want to say that something is the case, you cannot just leave it there. You have to select a form of the verb that indicates on what kind of evidence or supposition your statement is based.

Vive la différence

Appreciating difference is just one aspect of learning about language. This book will take you through the whole field, starting with the question of how it is that humans are able to speak at all (see The Birds and the Bees, page 10, and Human Evolution, page 14). Then you will look at how we actually make the sounds we do (see Voice and Speech, page 20). This will involve some unaccustomed but entertaining experimentation to feel what your throat and tongue and lips are actually doing when you speak. To talk about languages requires a sort of toolkit called linguistics, which is not about learning the rules of any one language, but about using certain techniques for classifying sounds (see Phonetics, page 24, and Phonology, page 28) and analysing words (see Morphology, page 34, and Lexicon, page 42) and the structure of sentences (see Syntax, page 46). You will then take a tour of the chief language groups in the world, which are sometimes arranged by family likeness and sometimes by geographical closeness (see pages 52–121).

"At any one time language is a kaleidoscope of styles, genres and dialects."
David Crystal

As language is above all a spoken phenomenon, there is deliberately no discussion of writing at this stage. This is kept back for a separate part of the book because writing is central to how we interact with not only the present, but also the past (see pages 128–59). Without it, we would not know most of what we do about the history of the world in general, or of languages in particular. Following on from this, you will be thinking about the tricky question of how languages differ from dialects (see page 162) and the pressing concerns of linguistic ecology and language death (see page 166). About half of the languages currently spoken will probably be extinct by the end of this century. The book concludes with a look at invented languages (see Artificial Languages, page 174) and what cautious predictions we might make about the future of the languages that survive into the 22nd century (see page 178).

If you know and love languages, this book is for you. If you are a relative newcomer to the subject, this is even more your book: the field is huge and rewarding. My hope is that people who are drawn to the subject will go out and learn another language. It's not simple or quick, but it can transform your world.

The hieroglyphs of ancient Egypt started out as a pictorial representation of things, but evolved to represent the sounds of the spoken language.

The Anatomy of Speech

It is often said that language is what makes us human. Whether it is all that makes us human is outside the scope of this book, but plainly humans talk in a way that non-human animals do not. You will see in the following sections that other animals have complex means of communication. You will also discover what it is about human physiology that makes us peculiarly well adapted for speech.

Evolutionary biologists and cognitive psychologists disagree about how far our capacity for language differs from that of other species. The serious question is how much of what enables human language had evolved before our earliest hominid ancestors (*Australopithecus*) separated off and went their own way to become *Homo habilis*, perhaps some 2 million years ago. Some experts maintain that all the evolutionary building blocks were in place before that time. Other specialists say that the important steps were taken only in the last million years or so. This is not simply a question of vocal cords and larynxes; it involves fundamental questions about the cognitive capacities of different sorts of mammalian brain.

The Birds and the Bees

The word *language* comes from Latin *lingua* (*tongue*) and language is primarily speech; writing is the recording of speech, and is the other side of the same coin. But speech came first.

Language is a form of communication; but not all forms of communication are language. If I raise an eyebrow at somebody eating smelly food on a bus or train, I have communicated disapproval, but I have not used language in the sense in which that word is normally used. If a man with a gun waves a white flag, we interpret this to indicate surrender, but this is not language either. If the fire alarm sounds, we know to evacuate the building without any word being spoken.

Dancing bees and singing birds

Non-human animals also have non-verbal forms of communication. Perhaps the best known is the "waggle dance" performed by honey bees within their hives. Bees that have been out foraging are able to communicate to those who remained behind the direction and distance they will have to travel in order to reach a particular source of food. These behaviours are extremely intricate. The life and death of the entire colony might depend on the accuracy of the communication, because if the bees abandon their hive and travel some distance to a location where a new source of food is reported, they will all die if that information is mistaken. It is thus of the highest evolutionary importance that they should have a reliable means of communication.

Bees can also buzz, but that has nothing to do with communication. Birds, on the other hand, can sing; that is more like human language. The fact that people refer to bird*song* shows that we intuit some similarity between the noises they make and what we do with our voices.

Birdsong plainly has some communicative content. Scientists have isolated the calls made

The use of a white banner as a flag of truce is described in the Hague Convention of 1899, but this signal of surrender dates back many centuries.

by different species to signal danger, for example, or to convey the message that they are ready for mating. These are generally quite short and simple. But there are also longer productions that can go on for many seconds or even minutes. In some species, an adult bird may have hundreds or even thousands of such songs. A bird known in North America as the brown thrasher has some 1,500 different songs. These are not simply random

The Anatomy of Speech

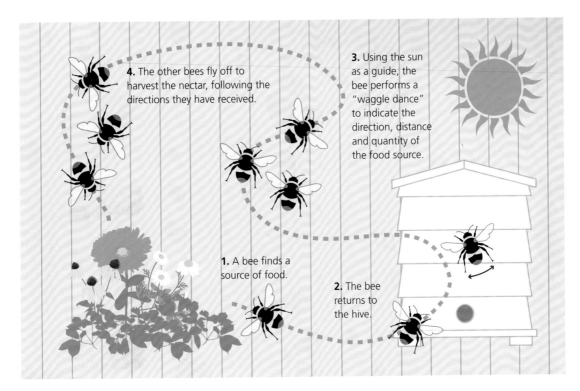

4. The other bees fly off to harvest the nectar, following the directions they have received.

3. Using the sun as a guide, the bee performs a "waggle dance" to indicate the direction, distance and quantity of the food source.

1. A bee finds a source of food.

2. The bee returns to the hive.

improvisations; studies of recordings show that they are repeated identically on other occasions.

It would be a mistake to suppose that these many thousands of avian songs are in some way equivalent to the myriad words that make up the vocabulary of a human language. It would appear that quite lengthy songs may mean no more than *here I am*: this may be for the purpose of attracting a mate, or in an aggressive sense to warn other birds not to trespass into the territory of the singer. Studies suggest that female birds are attracted to males with the largest repertoire of songs. This might be because they love music; more likely, the ability to produce many different kinds of song is equated with health and fitness.

Parrots are a special case. Although they do not of their own accord use human language between themselves, some species of parrot are able to mimic it very accurately and have even been found to practise in private. They have sufficient memory skills to associate objects with the names that humans give them, and to repeat these names on seeing the object. These instances

Brown thrashers are mimics, building up a huge repertoire of phrases by copying other birds.

of bird-to-human interaction can be written off as mimicry, but they have many characteristics of what we call language.

The songs of the sea

The most complex sonic performances among non-human animals are found among whales, dolphins and porpoises. These cetaceans are divided into toothed whales and baleen whales (who feed by filtering small creatures through plates of baleen – the same keratinous material of which our fingernails and hair are made). Baleen whales tend to be solitary and large; they do not have complex social structures but produce elaborate songs, particularly around mating time. Toothed whales live in groups; they do not have songs but use sound for social interactions. Toothed whales generally produce clicks and whistles; baleen whales produce clicks, tones, moans and a variety of other sounds. The frequency of baleen song is generally just below the threshold perceptible by

Like all members of the dolphin family, orcas communicate via a system of clicks and whistles. Orcas live in tightknit family groups, each of which has its own distinctive "accent".

The complex songs of male humpback whales change over time: when one whale adds a new phrase, the others learn it, too. Whale song was first recorded by microphones designed to detect Soviet submarines in the 1950s.

The Anatomy of Speech

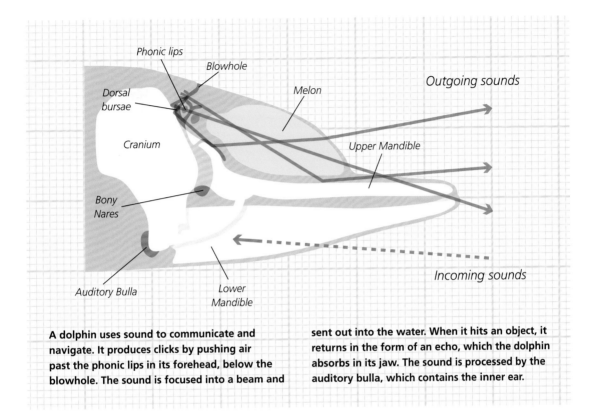

Phonic lips

Blowhole

Dorsal bursae

Melon

Outgoing sounds

Cranium

Upper Mandible

Bony Nares

Auditory Bulla

Lower Mandible

Incoming sounds

A dolphin uses sound to communicate and navigate. It produces clicks by pushing air past the phonic lips in its forehead, below the blowhole. The sound is focused into a beam and sent out into the water. When it hits an object, it returns in the form of an echo, which the dolphin absorbs in its jaw. The sound is processed by the auditory bulla, which contains the inner ear.

humans, while toothed whales use a broad range of frequencies, often far above the human range. Both can be detected using suitable hydrophonic equipment.

The humpback is a baleen whale. It can sing a song that lasts for half an hour or so and is made up of repeated phrases, each lasting for 10–20 seconds. The song, like its constituent phrases, may be repeated – for 20 hours or more by the same individual. Recordings over the years show that whale songs (unlike those of birds) are not exactly repeated, even if there are general similarities. The purpose of singing may be no more complex than attracting a mate. Among toothed whales, by contrast, more complex motivations may be at work. Dolphins have been found to possess memory skills comparable to that of some apes. It would appear that they use their clicks, whistles and other calls to communicate over distances of 10 kilometres (6 miles) or more about things such as the availability of food and the location of other members of the group. It would not be surprising if there were more to these communications than we currently appreciate. Creatures of such intelligence are likely to have interests that go beyond the mere acquisition of food and mates.

Human Evolution

Why are humans capable of so many varied sounds? Why are our languages such a rich repository of words for concrete and abstract things?

The first question has to do with the nature of our vocal apparatus, the second with the size and architecture of our brains. Differences are immediately apparent if we compare a modern human with, say, a rabbit – or even a chimpanzee. Much harder to answer is the question of how long speech has been around.

The brains of early humans

Anatomically modern human beings (*Homo sapiens sapiens*) probably evolved no more than 200,000 years ago. Evolutionary biologists agree that what is true of our anatomy now was more than likely true then. The first humans had all the apparatus necessary for speech. Whether they actually had spoken language 200,000 years ago is a question we cannot easily answer.

A slightly different question is whether earlier hominins, such as *Homo neanderthalensis*, were also capable of articulate and sustained speech.

Did *Homo erectus* have the capacity for language nearly 2 million years ago? In all these cases, what we are talking about is potential. Nobody can say with any certainty when that potential for language was first used.

These questions cannot be addressed by looking at written records; the earliest examples of writing that we have are barely 5,500 years old. Nobody seriously doubts that language must have existed long before the invention of writing, which presupposes that there is some language to be recorded. So anthropologists have to turn to the fossil record for clues. The problem here is that bones fossilize nicely, whereas soft tissues such as the brain, tongue and vocal cords leave no direct trace. However, it is possible to draw from what is preserved inferences about what is not.

For example, the skulls of our hominin predecessors might not contain fossil brains, but they contain the cavities in which those brains

Humans had the capacity for speech when *Homo sapiens sapiens* evolved 200,000 years ago, but we do not know when they first used it.

The Anatomy of Speech

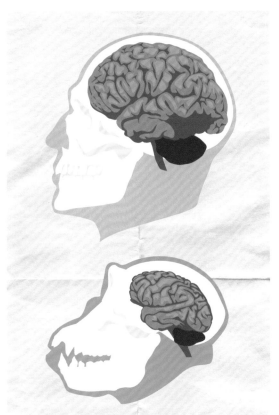

once sat. From their cubic capacity, it is possible to draw conclusions about the size of brains. Increased cerebral capacity relative to body size is an important element in the development of language. The brains of chimpanzees, our closest primate relatives, are typically a third the size of ours. They also have, relatively speaking, a smaller cerebral cortex, the area associated with problem solving, cognition and language.

But it would be a mistake to suppose that, since chimpanzees cannot speak and we can, the difference must be purely a question of the size and architecture of the brain. That is a necessary condition for the evolution of language, but it is not a sufficient one. You also need to have appropriate degrees of development of the vocal tract, from the larynx to the lips.

Lips, tongues and other muscles

It is also possible for forensic anthropologists to use their anatomical knowledge of humans and related species to draw further conclusions. For example, if they find a bony protuberance at a certain point, they might reasonably conclude that a particular type of muscle was attached to it in spite of the fact that those tissues are not represented in the fossil record. Most people are familiar with the way in which scientists are able to take a skull and use complex statistical techniques to work out what the face of its long-dead owner must have looked

The human brain is three times larger than that of a chimpanzee, but brain size alone is not enough for language to develop – the vocal tract has to be suitably evolved, too.

Forensic anthropologists are able to re-create a person's facial features based only on their skull. Applied to fossil skulls, these techniques indicate that 7 million years ago, our forebears already had lips that could potentially form speech.

like. From work of this kind, for example, it seems clear that all our hominin forebears up to 7 million years ago had lips of an appropriate thickness to be usefully manipulated for speech. But that is not enough by itself. Vocal cords are essential for human language and might have evolved at any time since *Homo erectus* 1.8 million years ago. Nothing can be said for certain beyond that anatomically modern *Homo sapiens* must always have had them throughout the 200,000-year history of the species.

There is also the question of breath control. Whereas chimpanzees make hoots that typically involve controlled exhalation for 5 seconds or so, human beings can generally sustain exhalations of anything from 5 to 12 seconds. Non-human primates are not capable of this level of articulatory control, which appears to have existed first in *Homo heidelbergensis*, about 800,000–200,000 years ago.

The tongue is, unsurprisingly, a critical element in language. Most vertebrates have them, from fish and reptiles to birds and mammals. But in humans the hyoid bone, to which the tongue is anchored, is farther down the throat. This means that there is more of the tongue in the throat than in other animals, where the longest part lies flat in the mouth. This presence of the tongue in the pharynx (the upper part of the throat near the root of the tongue) makes for a broader range of possible articulations. The vocal tract from pharynx to lips is effectively divided into two tubes: one runs from the pharynx to the glottis (the aperture between the vocal cords) and the second from the glottis to the lips. The tongue can be used to effect varying degrees of closure. What is important is that the range of sounds capable of being produced is at its largest when both tubes are of equal length. That feature does not seem to have evolved before *Homo sapiens*.

In conclusion, it would appear that our forebears have had the capacity for rudimentary language since *Homo habilis*, 2.4–1.8 million years ago. *Homo heidelbergensis* and Neanderthals were capable of a much wider range of sound from between 500,000 and 200,000 years ago. Even a liberal estimate would place the origin of recognizable language no earlier than that. But for the full range of sounds of which modern humans are capable we have to wait for the evolution of modern humans, approximately 200,000 years ago.

When these humans actually started to have complex languages of the kind attested in our

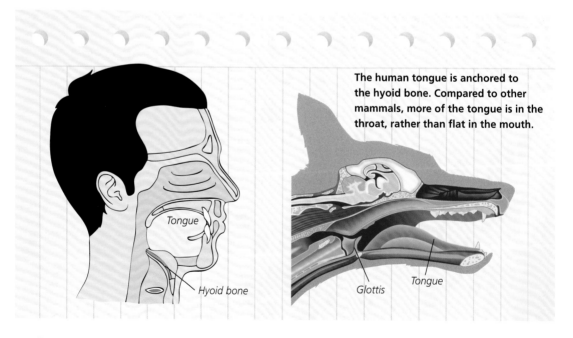

The human tongue is anchored to the hyoid bone. Compared to other mammals, more of the tongue is in the throat, rather than flat in the mouth.

Tongue

Hyoid bone

Glottis

Tongue

The Anatomy of Speech

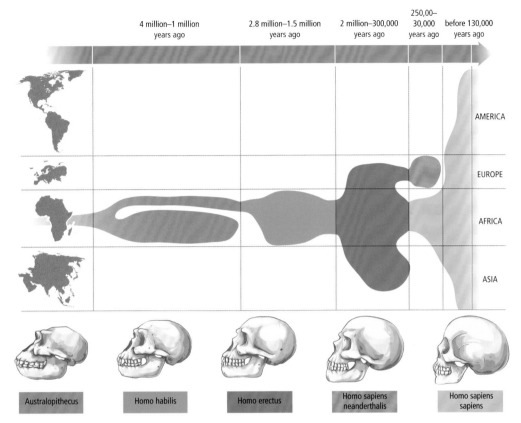

| 4 million–1 million years ago | 2.8 million–1.5 million years ago | 2 million–300,000 years ago | 250,00–30,000 years ago | before 130,000 years ago |

AMERICA

EUROPE

AFRICA

ASIA

| Australopithecus | Homo habilis | Homo erectus | Homo sapiens neanderthalis | Homo sapiens sapiens |

The timeline above shows the evolution of the human skull. The skull of the "Lucy" fossil, of the *Australopithecus* species, has a volume comparable to that of a chimpanzee.

earliest written records is unknowable. The earliest languages for which we have any evidence are those of Mesopotamia and Egypt, first recorded in the late 4th millennium BC. Writing presupposes that there are spoken words to write down, and it is reasonable to conclude that speech had been in place for tens, if not hundreds, of thousands of years before that. You will examine the history of recorded languages later in the book (see The Origins of Writing, page 130).

The puzzle of linguistic variety

Evolution poses an interesting problem for linguists. There has long been dispute over whether the first humans appeared in one place, the so-called Out of Africa theory, or evolved independently in a small number of locations in Africa and Asia. The modern consensus favours the former view. But in either case, if humans all started out in one or two places, how is it that modern humans speak something like 7,000 languages as different from each other as Irish and Chinese? Linguistic variety is as hard to explain as variety in the broader cultures of which languages form part. All we can say with any plausibility is that the difference must have been the result of groups getting larger and/or splitting up, so that forces that might have imposed uniformity, such as geography (a group is hemmed in by mountains) or groups sticking together for safety (wandering off to see what is beyond the next valley might get you killed) could not operate. We can imagine people splitting into groups and wandering across the globe with their languages evolving, even as their bodies no longer were.

What Makes Up a Language?

This is the part of the book where you are going to lift up the hood and look at the engine of language. Most people have the sense that language can be analysed at some level, even if much of what passes for analysis in the press and social media is little more than the parading of some people's prescriptive preferences about how others ought to speak and write. There is certainly a place for rules: in France, people drive on the right but in England on the left. If you decide to do your own thing, people will get hurt. To a lesser extent this is true of language: communication only works because groups agree to adhere to norms.

This book tries to describe how languages are, not prescribe how they ought to be. You will examine the units from which languages are made, from the smallest to the largest, beginning with sounds (phonetics and phonology), proceeding to the constituent parts of words (morphology), then on to the individual words (lexicon). You will finish by looking at grammar and syntax.

Voice and Speech

Human beings are unique among primates in the intricacy with which they can manipulate the phonatory and articulatory systems to produce an extraordinarily wide range of sounds.

The key to speech is the interplay between the phonatory system in the throat and the articulatory system in the head. The former comprises basically the larynx and vocal cords; the latter consists of the pharynx (which is just above the larynx), the oral cavity (the mouth, in other words) and the nasal cavity above.

Voicing vowels

The vocal cords within the larynx are under the conscious control of our somatic nervous system. They can be made to vibrate by being opened and closed in quick succession. When breath also passes through them, these vibrations are transferred to the outgoing stream of air. Linguists call this effect voice. If a voiced stream of air passes through the mouth without significant obstruction by the tongue, the result is a vowel sound. You can

try this at home: put the back of your hand in front of your mouth and say *ee* as in *wheel* followed by *a* as in *fast*. In both cases, you will feel the air coming out of your mouth. If you place your other hand on your larynx, you will feel the vibration that is voice. (Your larynx is approximately over your Adam's apple, which is present in both sexes but generally more prominent in men.) You will also notice that in the first case (*ee*), your tongue is high up in the front of your mouth; in the second (long *a*), the tongue is depressed and the sound is made at the back of the mouth. Now say *oo* as in *cool*. You can feel that rounding of the lips is another factor that conditions the kind of vowel sound that is made. Linguists have developed a complete system that allows all possible vowels to be plotted on a diagram (see opposite) and described in terms of open/close (whether the tongue is low or

Vibrating vocal cords in the larynx

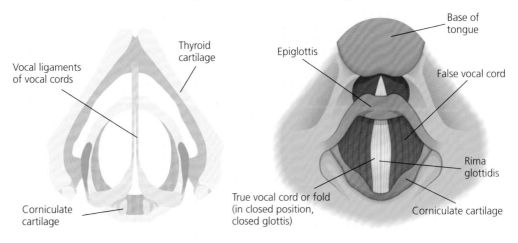

Vocal ligaments of vocal cords

Thyroid cartilage

Corniculate cartilage

Base of tongue

Epiglottis

False vocal cord

True vocal cord or fold (in closed position, closed glottis)

Rima glottidis

Corniculate cartilage

What Makes Up a Language?

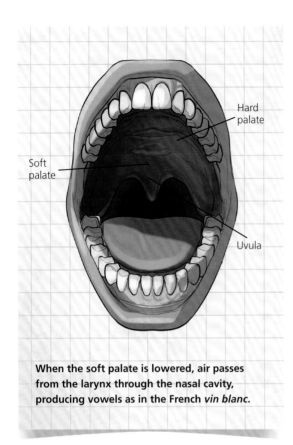

When the soft palate is lowered, air passes from the larynx through the nasal cavity, producing vowels as in the French *vin blanc*.

Soft palate

Hard palate

Uvula

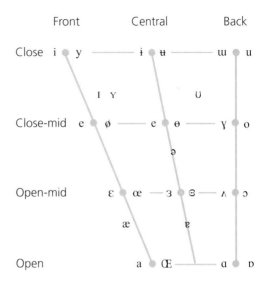

This diagram describes all possible vowels, in terms of how the sounds are formed. Where symbols appear in pairs, the one to the right represents a rounded vowel.

high), front/back (whether the highest part of the tongue is at the front or back of the mouth) and rounded/unrounded (whether the lips are pushed forward and into a circle) or not. The *ee* sound is a close, unrounded, front vowel; the long *a* of *fast* is an open, unrounded, back vowel; *oo* is a close, rounded, back vowel. We will look at this in more detail in the next section.

Some languages, such as French, have nasal vowels. When the air comes up from the larynx, it passes not into the mouth but up through the nasal cavity. It does this because the velum (or soft palate) is lowered. Most of the roof of your mouth is hard, but it becomes soft toward the back and you have muscular control over the resulting flap. Like a switch, it can be up or down. When it is down, a nasalized vowel is produced: in French *vin blanc*, both vowels are nasal. You can try this at home. Put a piece of paper in front of your lips, close your velum (you will be able to feel how to

do this) and say *unggg*. If the paper moves, you are not doing it right. If it stays still, you are making a nasal sound. Keeping the velum closed, put your hand under your nose and repeat the sound. You will feel air coming out through your nasal cavity.

Voicing consonants

Consonants are produced when the airstream is restricted by the pharynx or the tongue. If the air is completely restricted, you have a stop, for example *p, b, t, d, g, k, m, n*. Say *pan, ban, tan, Dan, man, nan* in English, or *Bad* (*bath*) in German or *bon* (*good*) in French. You will feel that in each case you are stopping off the airflow. If the air is partially restricted but not completely stopped, you have a fricative, for example *f, v, s, z, th, sh* as in *fail, veil, sin, zone, think, shine* in English, or *voll* (*full*) and *Weiss* (*white*) in German, or *fureur* (*rage*) and *vélo* (*bicycle*) in French. There are many others. If you make a stop and then quickly follow it with a fricative, you have an affricate: the first sound in English *George* and *jeans* is a mixture of the stop *d* and the fricative *zh*. French *Georges* and *je*, by contrast, begin with a pure fricative.

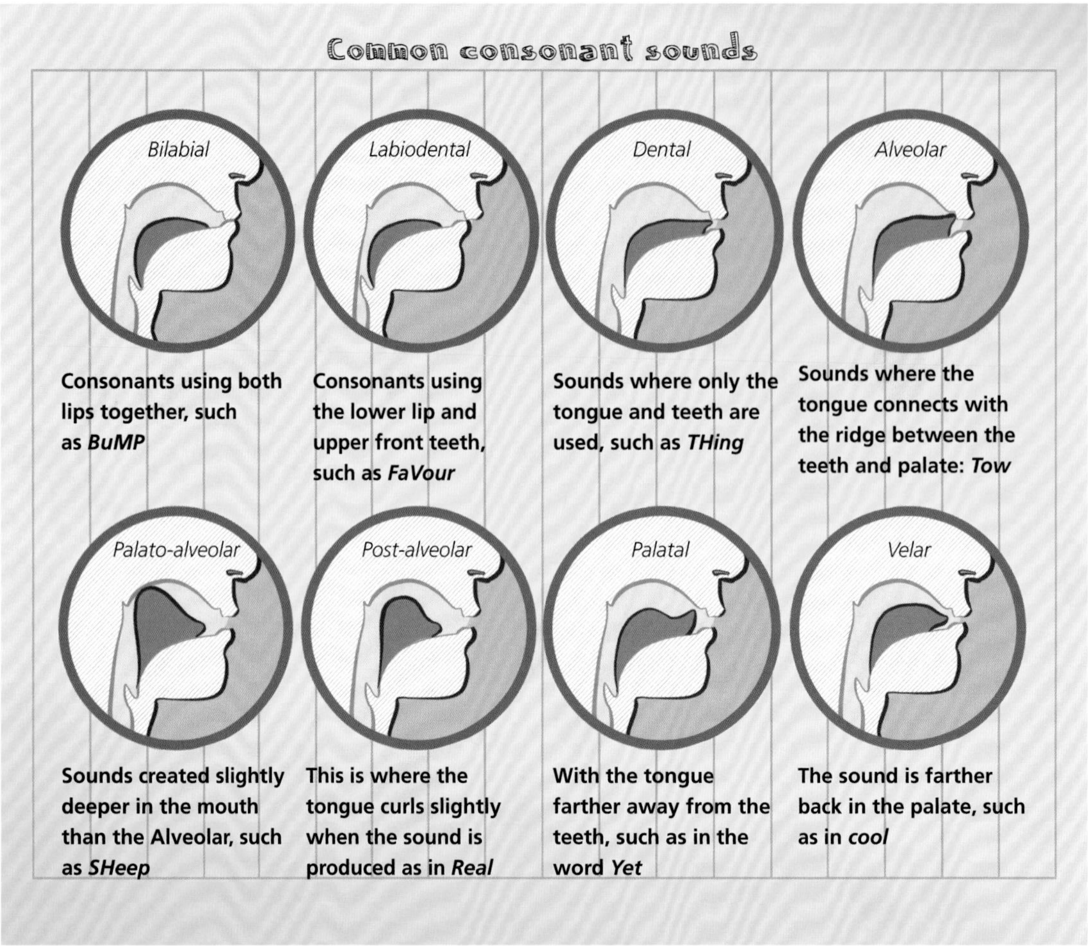

Bilabial
Consonants using both lips together, such as *BuMP*

Labiodental
Consonants using the lower lip and upper front teeth, such as *FaVour*

Dental
Sounds where only the tongue and teeth are used, such as *THing*

Alveolar
Sounds where the tongue connects with the ridge between the teeth and palate: *Tow*

Palato-alveolar
Sounds created slightly deeper in the mouth than the Alveolar, such as *SHeep*

Post-alveolar
This is where the tongue curls slightly when the sound is produced as in *Real*

Palatal
With the tongue farther away from the teeth, such as in the word *Yet*

Velar
The sound is farther back in the palate, such as in *cool*

Consonants are also classified in terms of how they are made, the relevant questions being:
1. Is there voice?
2. Where does the tongue meet the lips, teeth, alveolar ridge (just behind the teeth), hard palate or soft palate?
3. Is the airflow stopped or not?

Using this system we can say that the *t* in *talk* is a **voiceless alveolar** stop; *d* in *dark* is the voiced alternative. The *v* in *vote* is a voiced labiodental fricative (teeth meet lips); the *f* in *foot* is voiceless. The *t* in French *tuile* (*tile*) is a voiceless **dental** stop. The *d* in German *dunkel* (*dark*) is the voiced alternative. It is helpful to look at this in cross-section: the diagram above shows the articulation of some typical English, French and German sounds.

It will be evident that a huge range of sounds can be produced in this way, only a small number of which will actually be used in any given language.

Getting to grips with the details

A knowledge of phonetics, apart from being an interesting branch of speech science, can also help you to mimic more precisely the sounds of a foreign language and so sound less like a foreigner. Most English speakers never learn, for example, that the t-sounds in the French word *toilette* are dental (tip of tongue touches tip of teeth) whereas in the English *toilet* they are alveolar. Try it – it makes all the difference! Speakers of Italian likewise have difficulty with the French *un* because the vowel is nasalized, whereas the Italian *un* is not.

What Makes Up a Language?

The points of articulation

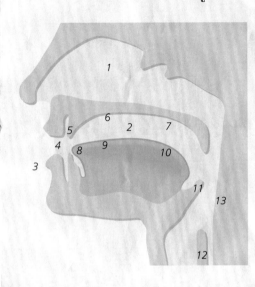

1. Nasal cavity
2. Oral cavity
3. Lips
4. Teeth
5. Alveolar ridge
6. Hard palate
7. Soft palate
8. Tip of the tongue
9. Blade of the tongue
10. Back of the tongue
11. Epiglottis
12. Vocal folds
13. Pharynx

A knowledge of phonetics can help you sound more like a local when you're speaking a foreign language.

Phonetics

In the last section, you looked at the mechanics of human articulation. It is worth pausing to say something about the means that linguists have used, and continue to use, in order to investigate and record sound.

Measuring vowels

In the British film *My Fair Lady* (1966), the hero is, perhaps surprisingly, a professor of phonetics. Not an obviously modest man, he declares that he can determine merely by a person's accent the street in London where he or she was born. So when Eliza Doolittle turns up, the challenge of making her talk like a member of the upper classes is irresistible. Early in the film, we see the professor and his friend Colonel Pickering listening to a recording. We hear something rather like a person saying *aaahhh* in the doctor's surgery during a throat examination. Higgins moves his tongue around in his mouth to vary the quality of the vowels. "How many vowel sounds do you think you heard altogether?" he asks. "I believe I counted twenty-four," replies Pickering. "Wrong by a hundred!" says Higgins. "What?" splutters the colonel. "To be exact you heard a hundred and thirty!" Higgins tells him. Pickering

is dumbfounded as Higgins seeks to demonstrate them with reference to a chart.

My Fair Lady was based on George Bernard Shaw's play *Pygmalion* (1913), and Professor Higgins is almost certainly based on Daniel Jones, who was at the time head of the Department of Phonetics at University College London. We have already seen that consonants can be classified by the place and manner of their articulation. Vowels are much harder to classify. Jones knew that, in order to make a vowel sound, the tongue must at some point be arched into a hump so that there will always be a point that is higher than the rest. He wanted to determine where that point lay for the different vowel sounds. So he went to St Bartholomew's Hospital in London in 1917. Lengthwise along his tongue he arranged a small chain made of tiny lead plates (see opposite). He then spoke the various vowels, and while doing so had his head X-rayed by Dr H Trevelyan George. The use of the chain was a brilliant solution to the problem of how to image the tongue, given that soft tissue does not show up on X-rays.

The eight cardinal vowels

The number of potential vowel sounds that a human can make is extremely large. Not all languages use all or even most of these. But it is scientifically important to have a means of classifying them. Daniel Jones made the great step forward of identifying eight cardinal vowels. He arranged these in a quadrilateral, the points

Professor Higgins, a professor of phonetics, uses a chart to demonstrate the wide variety of possible vowel sounds to his friend Pickering in *My Fair Lady*.

What Makes Up a Language?

on which were supposed to correspond roughly to positions within the mouth and to indicate the position adopted by the highest part of the tongue during the articulation of that vowel. When dealing with any language, it is possible to plot where its vowel sounds fall by using Jones's diagram (see right). Some might be identical to the cardinal vowels; others may be plotted with a dot showing where they fall in relation to these known points so that a suitably trained person can reproduce the sounds as closely as possible. Jones's cardinal vowels delineate the outer contours of what is possible in the production of any vowel; they are convenient landmarks that allow other vowels to be identified by reference to them.

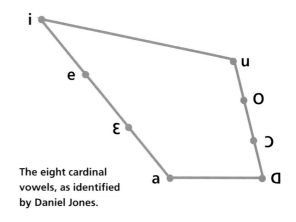

The eight cardinal vowels, as identified by Daniel Jones.

Measuring consonants

For the investigation of consonantal articulation, Jones favoured the palatogram. This involved

having a dentist make an artificial palate for a person, made to fit the mouth exactly. It would be coloured black and some finely powdered chalk would be applied to the entire surface before it was inserted into the mouth. The subject would then

Daniel Jones, the real Professor Higgins

In order to determine as precisely as possible the position of the tongue when making vowel sounds, Daniel Jones, head of the Department of Phonetics at University College London in the 1910s, arranged for his own head to be X-rayed while he was speaking.

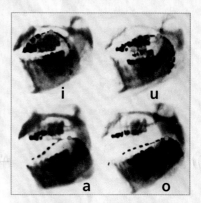

As soft tissue such as the tongue does not show up on X-rays, Jones made use of a technique pioneered before the First World War by E A Meyer, which involved placing a chain made of lead plates on his tongue. The chain can be clearly seen in the images above, outlining the changing shape of the tongue.

articulate a consonant and the palate would be removed. The areas from which chalk was missing would indicate the area where the moist tongue had made contact with the artificial palate. The technique has changed little over time except that, instead of chalk, the surface of the artificial palate is nowadays covered with tiny electrodes. When the tongue makes contact with any of these, a signal is sent to an external monitor, which provides the same information far more quickly and reliably than looking for missing chalk. This method is called electropalatography.

Another technique favoured by modern phoneticians in investigating the nature of articulation is the spectrogram. This is the output from a device called a spectrograph, which measures sound in the form of a continuous print-out or display, with time on the horizontal axis and frequency on the vertical. The overall amount of energy in any articulation is marked by the amount of light and dark on display. This technique existed before the age of modern electronics. The kymograph had a membrane to detect sound vibrations and a needle to record them on a rotating cylinder.

If phoneticians are to be able to communicate the results of their investigations to others, they need some kind of written system that is as

In the past, artifical palates covered in chalk were used to study the position of the tongue when forming consonants. Today, electrodes record this information.

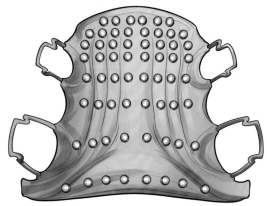

unambiguous as possible. It is notoriously hard to capture the subtleties of sound using the ordinary Roman alphabet. For one thing, it is used differently by speakers of different languages. For another, even among speakers of one language, you cannot be sure that everyone will understand the same sound because of differences between dialects.

The International Phonetic Alphabet

While it is, for all kinds of reasons, not possible to devise a system of writing in which one symbol denotes only one sound, we can get a great deal closer to writing a language without using the Roman alphabet. The solution is called the International Phonetic Alphabet (see opposite). For consonants, it involves drawing up a table with place of articulation running along the horizontal axis from the front of the mouth to the back (bilabial, labiodental, dental, alveolar, post-alveolar, retroflex, palatal, velar, uvular, pharyngeal, laryngeal) and method of articulation running vertically (stop, nasal, trill, tap, fricative, lateral fricative, approximant, lateral approximant) in voiced and unvoiced varieties. It is not feasible to explain all of these here; anyone who is interested can easily pursue the topic by searching the web or consulting the sources recommended in this book (see Bibliography, page 184).

The point is that such an arrangement produces an enormous number of possibilities. Of these, some are found in many languages (for example, the voiceless dental stop [t], although not in English); others are much rarer (for example, the alveolar trill fricative, found chiefly in Czech, where it is written ř); other boxes in the International Phonetic Alphabet chart are left empty because, although phoneticians judge that the sound is possible, it is not found in any known human language (for example, a palatal trill); other boxes are shaded in because it is judged that the resultant sound would be physically impossible, rather than just rare or difficult (such as a nasal pharyngeal, because if both the pharynx and nasal passage are closed no sound at all can escape).

What Makes Up a Language?

THE INTERNATIONAL PHONETIC ALPHABET (revised to 2015)

CONSONANTS (PULMONIC)

© 2015 IPA

	Bilabial	Labiodental	Dental	Alveolar	Postalveolar	Retroflex	Palatal	Velar	Uvular	Pharyngeal	Glottal
Plosive	p b			t d		ʈ ɖ	c ɟ	k ɡ	q ɢ		ʔ
Nasal	m	ɱ		n		ɳ	ɲ	ŋ	N		
Trill	ʙ			r					ʀ		
Tap or Flap		ⱱ		ɾ		ɽ					
Fricative	ɸ β	f v	θ ð	s z	ʃ ʒ	ʂ ʐ	ç ʝ	x ɣ	χ ʁ	ħ ʕ	h ɦ
Lateral fricative				ɬ ɮ							
Approximant		ʋ		ɹ		ɻ	j	ɰ			
Lateral approximant				l		ɭ	ʎ	ʟ			

Symbols to the right in a cell are voiced, to the left are voiceless. Shaded areas denote articulations judged impossible.

CONSONANTS (NON-PULMONIC)

Clicks	Voiced implosives	Ejectives
ʘ Bilabial	ɓ Bilabial	' Examples:
ǀ Dental	ɗ Dental/alveolar	p' Bilabial
ǃ (Post)alveolar	ʄ Palatal	t' Dental/alveolar
ǂ Palatoalveolar	ɠ Velar	k' Velar
ǁ Alveolar lateral	ʛ Uvular	s' Alveolar fricative

OTHER SYMBOLS

ʍ Voiceless labial-velar fricative

w Voiced labial-velar approximant

ɥ Voiced labial-palatal approximant

ʜ Voiceless epiglottal fricative

ʢ Voiced epiglottal fricative

ʡ Epiglottal plosive

ɕ ʑ Alveolo-palatal fricatives

ɺ Voiced alveolar lateral flap

ɧ Simultaneous ʃ and x

Affricates and double articulations can be represented by two symbols joined by a tie bar if necessary.

t͡s k͡p

VOWELS

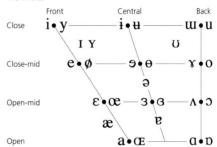

Front   Central   Back

Close: i•y — ɨ•ʉ — ɯ•u

ɪ ʏ   ʊ

Close-mid: e•ø — ɘ•ɵ — ɤ•o

ə

Open-mid: ɛ•œ — ɜ•ɞ — ʌ•ɔ

æ   ɐ

Open: a•ɶ — ɑ•ɒ

Where symbols appear in pairs, the one to the right represents a rounded vowel.

SUPRASEGMENTALS

ˈ	Primary stress	ˌfoʊnəˈtɪʃən
ˌ	Secondary stress	
ː	Long	eː
ˑ	Half-long	eˑ
˘	Extra-short	ĕ
ǀ	Minor (foot) group	
‖	Major (intonation) group	
.	Syllable break	ɹi.ækt
‿	Linking (absence of a break)	

DIACRITICS

Some diacritics may be placed above a symbol with a descender, e.g. ŋ̊

̥	Voiceless	n̥ d̥	̤	Breathy voiced	b̤ a̤	̪	Dental	t̪ d̪
̬	Voiced	s̬ t̬	̰	Creaky voiced	b̰ a̰	̺	Apical	t̺ d̺
ʰ	Aspirated	tʰ dʰ	̼	Linguolabial	t̼ d̼	̻	Laminal	t̻ d̻
̹	More rounded	ɔ̹	ʷ	Labialized	tʷ dʷ	̃	Nasalized	ẽ
̜	Less rounded	ɔ̜	ʲ	Palatalized	tʲ dʲ	ⁿ	Nasal release	dⁿ
̟	Advanced	u̟	ˠ	Velarized	tˠ dˠ	ˡ	Lateral release	dˡ
̠	Retracted	e̠	ˤ	Pharyngealized	tˤ dˤ	̚	No audible release	d̚
̈	Centralized	ë	̴	Velarized or pharyngealized	ɫ			
̽	Mid-centralized	ɛ̽	̝	Raised	e̝ (ɹ̝ = voiced alveolar fricative)			
̩	Syllabic	n̩	̞	Lowered	e̞ (β̞ = voiced bilabial approximant)			
̯	Non-syllabic	e̯	̘	Advanced Tongue Root	e̘			
˞	Rhoticity	ɚ a˞	̙	Retracted Tongue Root	e̙			

TONES AND WORD ACCENTS

LEVEL			CONTOUR		
e̋ or ˥	Extra high		ě or ˩˥	Rising	
é ˦	High		ê ˥˩	Falling	
ē ˧	Mid		e̋ ˧˥	High rising	
è ˨	Low		e̗ ˩˧	Low rising	
ȅ ˩	Extra low		e̞ ˧˩˧	Rising-falling	
ꜜ Downstep			↗ Global rise		
ꜛ Upstep			↘ Global fall		

Typefaces: Doulos SIL (metatext); Doulos SIL, IPA Kiel, IPA LS Uni (symbols)

Phonology

The study of the sounds that occur in language is called phonology. A *phone* is a single speech sound, while a *phoneme* is a *phone* whose replacement by a different one would alter the meaning of a word.

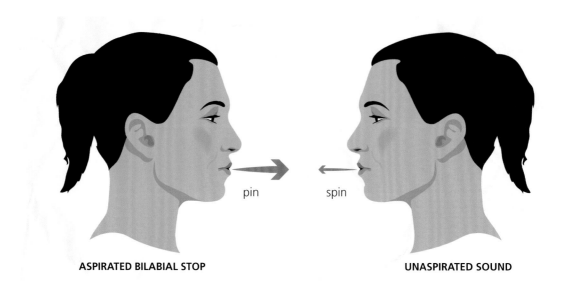

pin   spin

ASPIRATED BILABIAL STOP   **UNASPIRATED SOUND**

If an English speaker says the word *pin*, a puff of breath accompanies the first consonant. Linguists call this an aspirated bilabial stop. But if the same speaker says the word *spin*, that little puff of breath is absent or much reduced; this is an unaspirated sound. If English is your native language, you can try this by putting a piece of paper in front of your lips and watching it move, or not, as you pronounce these two words. So there are two different sounds here: [pʰ] and [p] respectively.

Linguists call any given sound a phone and use square brackets to represent it. In this example, the difference in sound is not very important. If a non-native speaker were to pronounce the word *pin* with [p] rather than [pʰ], she would still be understood. Consider the initial consonants in *keep* and *cool*; the first one is pronounced forward in the mouth (palatal) whereas the second one is farther

back (**velar**). But they are so similar that it would not matter if someone mixed them up.

Voicing and phonemes

Now consider a different phonetic feature: voicing. We have seen that a voiceless consonant is made when the vocal cords are not vibrating, whereas a voiced one is accompanied by resonance of the cords: thus [pʰ] is a voiceless bilabial stop, whereas [bʰ] is the voiced alternative. They are both always aspirated when they are the first sound in the word, so there is no difference there. Say *pin*; now say *bin*. What happens if you substitute [bʰ] for [pʰ] in the first word? You get confusion – you can no longer tell apart a *pin* from a *bin*.

In the same way, in French it is important to differentiate between *pain* (bread) and *bain* (bath). So whereas aspiration does not affect meaning very

What Makes Up a Language?

much in English and French, voicing does. If you ignore it, you get chaos.

Pin and *bin* are known as minimal pairs. These are words in which changing just a single sound changes the meaning. Linguists say that voicing is phonemic in English: it makes a difference to meaning rather than just sound. An inventory of all such significant alternations found in minimal pairs makes up the set of English phonemes. A *phone* is any discrete speech sound; a *phoneme* is a *phone* whose replacement by a different *phone* would alter the meaning of a word. Whereas a phone is written in square brackets, a phoneme is written between forward slashes. Whether you pronounce [pʰɪn] or [pɪn], both are understood by English speakers as varieties of the same phoneme, /p/; whether you say [cʰiːp] (as in the English *keep*) or [kuːl] (as in the English *cool*), they are still just varieties of the phoneme /k/.

In other languages, different features will be phonemic. In Ancient Greek, for example, it mattered very much whether you said [p] or [pʰ]: the word *ponos* means *labour*, whereas *phonos* means *murder*. It is important not to confuse these. So for the ancient Greeks /p/ and /ph/ were phonemes; for English speakers there is only /p/, which is pronounced as [ph] at the start of a word

and [p] in all other places. When two different phones are basically just aspects of the same phoneme differently realized in different phonetic environments, they are called **allophones**. In Greek, /p/ and /ph/ are not allophones.

Consonant clusters

If a speaker of Arabic asks you the way to Westminster Abbey, she will almost always pronounce it as *Westminister*, inserting a vowel where there ought not to be one. There is a reason for this. The cluster *-nst-* is not found in Arabic (a cluster is a group of two or more consonants). In fact, you will never find any clusters of three consonants. Arabic permits clusters with two components, but not three. So the name *Mustafa* is allowed, but not **Munstafa* (the asterisk indicates a non-existent form).

In Spanish, words cannot begin **st-* or **sp-* (unless they have been borrowed from a foreign language). Thus English has *stupid*, *splendid*, French has *stupide*, *splendide* but Spanish has *estúpido*, *espléndido*. But French does not always side with English in this respect. Whereas English has *study*, French has *étude*, which must derive from an earlier **estude*; and where English people

Allophones

In German, the classic example of an allophone is the difference between the *ich-Laut* and the *ach-Laut*. After a front vowel, as in *ich* or *mich* (*I* or *me*), we get a sound realized as a voiceless palatal fricative, represented by the symbol [ç] in the International Phonetic Alphabet. After a back vowel, it appears as a voiceless velar fricative or [x] in words such as *Buch* (book) or the interjection *ach* (oh!).

Different languages make different shapes, as you can see from the German, Italian, English and Polish examples above.

say *spine* (of something sharp), the French say *épine*, from **espine*.

Syllables and sound structures

All languages have implicit conventions governing which sequences of sound are permitted and which are not. These are called phonotactic rules. Alongside surface features, such as the phonemic inventory of a language and its patterns of intonation, phonotactic rules are what give a language its characteristic shape and feel at a deeper level. One of the ways we can appreciate this most clearly is by thinking about the overall shapes of words in different languages. Consider English *chair, friend, strong, tooth, weather* next to German *Stuhl, Freund, stark, Zahn, Wetter*, Italian *sedia, amico, forte, dente, tempo*, Turkish *iskemle, arkadaş, kuvvetli, diş, hava*, and Polish *krzesło, przyjaciel, mocny, ząb, pogoda*. What is striking is not just how different these languages are in their roots – *friend* and *Freund* are obviously related,

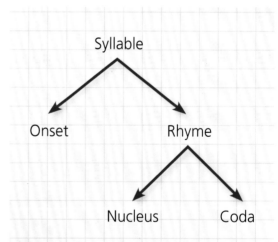

A syllable is a sound that can stand alone or with others to make a word. In the latter case, the component units of the word are called syllables. A syllable may be further analysed as shown in the diagram above.

What Makes Up a Language?

whereas *arkadaş* and *przyjaciel* are not – but how different they are in shape. The Italian words have a lilting structure, which is partly a result of the intonation patterns of Italian, but also a product of phonotactic rules. English and German have more stolid-sounding words like *strong*, *stark*, *tooth*, *Zahn*. Spanish, as we have seen, cannot begin a word with **st-*.

What I have been calling "shape" is largely about what form a syllable is allowed to take. A syllable is hard to define but relatively easy to understand if I say that English *potato* is made up of three syllables: *po - ta - to*. At its fullest, a syllable is made up of an onset and a rhyme: in English *spin*, for example, the onset is [sp] and the rhyme is [ɪn]. The rhyme is further divided up into the nucleus (in this case [ɪ]) and the coda (in this case [n]). In English, a syllable does not have to have an onset: words like *in*, *on*, *up* have no onset, only rhymes. A word like *eye* is pure nucleus; forget the spelling – there is only the vowel sound [aɪ] and no coda. There is likewise only a nucleus in Italian *è* (*it is*), English *a*, Latin *ī* (*go!*).

In Arabic, by contrast, every word must have an onset: no word, of whatever length, is allowed to begin with a vowel. If we think about a word like Arabic *'anā* (*I*), it might look and sound to many foreign listeners as though it starts with an *a*-vowel, but it does not. It starts with a glottal stop – a voiceless stop made by constricting the airflow at the glottis, that is, at the aperture in the vocal cords (as in German *der Adler*, meaning *the eagle*). In the IPA the glottal stop is represented by [ʔ]. It is indicated in English transcription *'anā* with an apostrophe and in Arabic (see below) by the letter *'alif* (the vertical letter on the right) and the so-called *hamzat al-qat* (the small character above the *'alif* that resembles a mirrored 2):

This gives Arabic a very different sound from English or Italian.

If a syllable has no coda, it is said to be open. Every syllable in the English word *po-ta-to*, in the Italian *a-mi-co* and in the Polish *o-bo-ra* is open. But whereas most Italian syllables are open, the same is not true for Polish. An English word like *strands* not only has an onset, nucleus and coda, but also has clusters at its beginning and end. If we write C for any consonant and V for any vowel, this means that the word has the shape CCCVCCC.

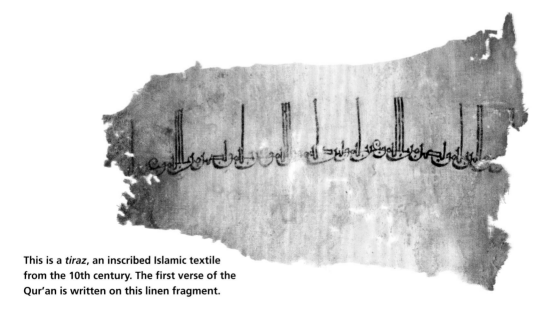

This is a *tiraz*, an inscribed Islamic textile from the 10th century. The first verse of the Qur'an is written on this linen fragment.

The maximum number of phones that English permits in the coda is four: *glimpsed* has the shape CCVCCCC. (Ignore the spelling, as always; it is pronounced [glɪmpst].)

Japanese, on the other hand, has a very different structure. Most syllables have no coda. Those that do are found in the context of a vowel, followed either by a doubled consonant (which serves as the coda to one syllable and the onset of the next one) or by a nasal consonant. Article 1 of the Universal Declaration of Human Rights in Japanese looks like this (transcribed into Roman letters, with hyphens marking syllable boundaries within words): *Su-be-te no nin-gen wa, u-ma-re-na-ga-ra ni shi-te ji-yū de a-ri, kat-su, son-gen to ken-ri to ni tsui-te byō -dō de a-ru. Nin-gen wa, ri-sei to ryō-shin to o sa-zu-ke-ra-re-te o-ri, ta-gai ni dō-hō no sei-shinn o mot-te kō-dō shi-na-ke-re-ba na-ra-na*i. ("All human beings are born free and equal in dignity and rights. They are endowed with reason and conscience and should act towards one another in a spirit of brotherhood.") You can appreciate at once that most of the syllables in this utterance are open. A quick calculation shows the precise figure to be 85 percent. This creates a very different texture from that of English or German or Turkish or Arabic or Russian.

Sonority hierarchies

An important factor in determining the shape of a syllable is resonance of individual sounds. If you say a vowel sound, for example, it has more acoustic power than a consonant. Try it. Say *a, o, u*. Now say *p, t*. Do it again. The vowels carry farther; any singer knows this from experience. Sounds can be arranged in what linguists call a sonority hierarchy. This is broadly applicable across different languages, but they may differ in the weight that they give to such considerations. The hierarchy for English is shown in the diagram below.

In general, one expects the nucleus of a syllable to be either a vowel or a semi-vowel. So the German words *ich bin müde* [ɪç bɪn myːdə] (*I am tired*) all have vowels as their nuclei; the last word is made of two syllables, both with vowel nuclei. In Czech, a place name like *Brno* appears hard to pronounce. But it is made of two syllables: Br-no. [br-noʊ]. The *r* is classified as a semi-vowel because

Sounds can be arranged in order of their acoustic power. This illustration shows the sonority hierarchy for English.

What Makes Up a Language?

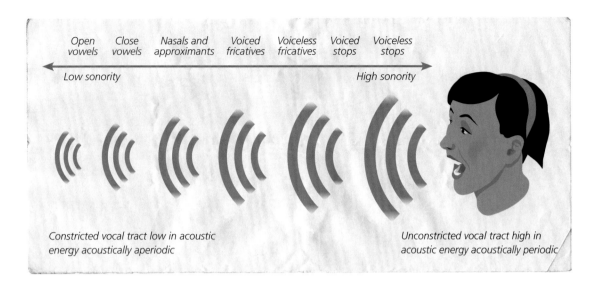

Open vowels	Close vowels	Nasals and approximants	Voiced fricatives	Voiceless fricatives	Voiced stops	Voiceless stops

Low sonority   High sonority

Constricted vocal tract low in acoustic energy acoustically aperiodic

Unconstricted vocal tract high in acoustic energy acoustically periodic

it has some of the characteristics of a vowel and some of a consonant: in any given context, it will unmask itself and perform as one or the other. This can function as the nucleus of a syllable; it has a quality of its own. It is less sonorous than, for example, *Bruno*, but still has an articulable nucleus. English has syllabic resonants of this same kind in words like *apple* and *button*. As always, forget the spelling; they are pronounced [æpl] and [bʌtn]. The nucleus of the second syllable of each word is not a vowel, but *l* and *n* respectively. Such sequences are treated as sufficiently sonorous in English and so permitted by the rules.

Now imagine you are given the sounds *p, l, a* and asked to arrange them into a syllable. You might make the real words *pal, lap, alp*. The arrangement *pla-* is not found by itself but is acceptable in a word like *planet*. What English would not allow is a word **lpa*; you cannot have *p* as the nucleus of a syllable in English because it is one of the least sonorous sounds there is. In the same way, the sequence *trans* is possible

in a number of languages whereas **rtasn* is unimaginable. This is because the sequencing principle requires the more sonorous elements to be closest to the nucleus, while the less sonorous ones are relegated to the margins of the syllable in a uniformly decreasing slope.

TRANS

NOT ....

RTASN

This sequencing principle is of wide, but not universal, application. In the Berber dialect Imdlawn Tashlhiyt, the word *tftktstt* is found. It means *you sprained it*. Linguists analyse it as three syllables, *tf.tk.tstt*, so that you find *f, k, s* as syllabic nuclei – something that does not happen too commonly in most other known languages! Only the second syllable violates the sequencing rule, since *k* and *t* are of equal sonority.

Morphology

Do you think you know what a word is? This might sound like the sort of question to which everyone knows the answer, but the concept of the word is actually quite hard to define.

You might say that a word is one of those things that this page is covered in, made up of a group of black letters with a space at the beginning and end. This sort of "I know it when I see it" approach works well enough, especially in your own native language. It gets more complicated if you look at enough examples from languages quite different from those of western Europe. Most linguists would say that a word is the smallest unit of speech (or writing) that can stand by itself and convey some sort of information. The German word *Pferd* (*horse*) is an example, but so is *das* (*the*) – the latter tells you that the word that follows it is definite rather than indefinite. You have examined the smallest significant units of sound (phonemes) and you are now going to look at the smallest units of meaning. You will see that, although the word is the smallest item that can stand by itself, many words can themselves be analysed into smaller constituent parts that also convey meaning, whether or not they are able to stand alone as words in their own right.

Long words and compounds

You can begin by observing that some languages have very long words. *Antidisestablishmentarianism* is often held up as the longest word in English (whether it is or not is a different question). The German *Donaudampfschifffahrtselektizitäten-hauptbetriebswerkbauunterbeamtengesellschaft* is recorded by the *Guinness Book of Records* as

This 80-letter name of a probably made-up organization is in the record books, but not the dictionary. The longest German word in everyday usage is *Kraftfahrzeug-Haftpflichtversicherung*, (motor vehicle liability insurance), with 36 letters.

What Makes Up a Language?

LLANFAIRPWLLGWYNGYLLGOGERYCHWYRNDROBWLLLLANTYSILIOGOGOGOCH

Llan-vire-pooll-guin-gill-go-ger-u-queern-drob-ooll-llandus-ilio-gogo-goch

The name of this Welsh village was invented in the 1860s purely so that the local railway station would have the longest name – and sign – of any station in Britain. The village is known locally as Llanfair, or Llanfair PG.

the longest word in that language, meaning "association for subordinate officials of the head office management of the Danube steamboat electrical services." One imagines that such a word does not crop up very often, except in discussions about long words. It might be a party trick to be able to say it, like Welsh *Llanfairpwllgwyngyll-gogerychwyrndrobwllllantysiliogogogoch*, which apparently means "St Mary's church in the hollow of the white hazel near to the rapid whirlpool of Llantysilio of the red cave." As names for railway stations go, it is far more evocative than most.

But all of these long words are still just words. They are single units of utterance. Furthermore, they could be substituted for *X* in the sentence *Do you know anything about X?* In this question, X could be *golf*, or *antidisestablishmentarianism* or the Welsh railway station with the long name. In Turkish, on the other hand, there is a word *avruplılaştırılamıyanlardansınız*, which means "You are one of those who cannot be Europeanized." It too is a single utterance: you take a deep breath and say it and then move on to the next word. But it is also unlike the other examples that we have seen: you could not substitute it for X in

the example of the question given above. This is because Turkish manages to roll up into one word what in most other languages you would need an entire sentence to say.

These curiosities are perennially rich sources of material for setters of general knowledge quizzes, but there is a serious point to them as well. The German and Welsh examples are actually quite straightforward: they involve welding together a number of freestanding words to form a longer freestanding compound. The Turkish example is quite different, since the elements of which it is composed cannot stand by themselves.

In German, compounding is quite normal. You can say *Rathausbalkon* as one word. The English equivalent is *town hall balcony*. That looks and sounds like three independent words, but they are taken together as one entity. English is actually getting a result that is very similar to German, but it stops short of the decisive step of physically joining the words together on the page. We might call these pseudo-compounds. In spoken English, some of these pseudo-compounds probably sound very much like one string of speech. A phrase like *Post Office Savings* can be enunciated with very

VIOLIN

A morpheme is the smallest unit of meaning, smaller than a word: it can be attached to verbs or nouns to create new, related words, but it cannot exist on its own.

VIOLIN-IST

little pause between its constituent parts so that it sounds like *Postofficesavings*. In French, on the other hand, such a thing would be quite out of the question. You would be obliged to render *the town hall balcony* as *le balcon de l'hôtel de ville*. *Town hall* has to be *the hall of town* and *town hall balcony* has to be *the balcony of the hall of town*. English and German are content to compound by mere juxtaposition, whereas French is not satisfied without the glue provided by *de*, meaning *of*, even where this involves repeating it a few times.

Morphemes

Rat, *Haus* and *Balkon* exist by themselves as words meaning *council*, *house* and *balcony*. English *antidisestablishmentarianism* is more complicated: *anti-*, *dis-*, and *-ism* are not elements that can stand by themselves as words. In French *tricher* means *to cheat* and *tricheur* is *a person who cheats*; *-eur* has no independent existence. It is something you use to indicate a person who does an action. In English there is a verb *conduct* and a noun *conductor*. You can add endings to nouns as well: thus *violin*, *violinist*. The elements *-eur*, *-or* and *-ist* are units of meaning, smaller than a word and an essential part of the make-up and meaning of the word.

All of these things are examples of a morpheme. The use of a morpheme like *-ist* to create a new but related word is an example of derivational morphology. The use of a morpheme like *-ed* to mark the past tense (*dream* : *dreamed*) is part of inflectional morphology. Morphemes that cannot exist as independent words are called bound; morphemes that can exist independently are called free – for example, both elements in German *Buchhandlung* (*book shop*) or English *doorman*.

Perhaps the most obvious bound morpheme in English is the plural marker /s/: *cat* vs. *cats*, *dog* vs. *dogs*, *house* vs. *houses*. Even here, though, phonology makes its influence felt. Although the morpheme looks the same in spelling, there are three different phonetic realizations: [s] in *cats*, [z] in *dogs* and [ɪz] in *houses*. Depending on the last sound in the noun, you will have a differently pronounced plural marker (allomorph). This is an example of the intersection of phonology and morphology called morphophonology (or morphophonemics).

But the morpheme *-s* is also found in English verbal endings. Compared with many other languages, English verbal morphology is very simple: *I speak, you speak, s/he speaks, we speak, you*

What Makes Up a Language?

speak, they speak. All these forms look and sound the same except for the form used for he (the so-called third person singular). In French we find *je parle, tu parles, il parle, nous parlons, vous parlez, ils parlent*. The system is more complex, but we can still describe the endings *-e, -es, -e, -ons, -ez, -ent* as morphemes added to the basic verbal stem *parl-*.

Not everything needs to be added to the end of the word. In German, the verb *kaufen* (*to buy*) has a past participle *ge-kauf-t* (*bought*) with *-t* at the end and *ge-* at the beginning. A form added to the beginning of a word is a prefix and one added to the end is a suffix. Both are examples of affixes, which just means something added somewhere to a word.

Another kind of affix is the infix, which is a morpheme that appears inside another word, not at the beginning or end. In the sequence CVXC, X is an infix. In Ancient Greek, a root *lab-* means take. The past tense, *he took*, is *elabe*. But the present tense involves two nasal infixes: *he takes* is la-**m**-b-**an**-ei. The two infixes are in bold to make them easier to see here.

Ablaut

But what about something like English *sing, sang, sung*? You might be tempted to think that there are morphemes *-i-, -a-, -u-* that you use to mark different forms. The parallel with *sink, sank, sunk* looks convincing. But then why do we not get *think, *thank, *thunk* but *think, thought, thought*? And why does the separate verb *thank* form its past with a [t] (written *-ed*): *thanked*? A glance at forms like *seek, sought* or *think, thought* or *take, took* reveals that something else is going on. The phenomenon is called ablaut, and is found in other languages, such as the German *werben* (*to advertise*), with the forms *wirbt* (*s/he advertises*), *warb* (*s/he advertised*), *geworben* (*advertised*). Its

English verbal morphology is relatively simple, with fewer different endings than French.

je parle
I speak

tu parles
you speak

il parle
he speaks

nous parlons
we speak

roots are complicated but it can be encapsulated as a form of morphological marking that is not done by a discrete morpheme like -ed, but by the alternation of vowels.

You can have ablaut distinction and bound morphemes occurring together in the same word. In Ancient Greek, leip-o means I leave. The leip-part is called the present stem and the -o indicates that I am doing the action (not you or he or they). Contrast with this the form le-loip-a, which means I have left. You can see immediately that leip- differs from -loip- by an alternation of e with o, rather like English get vs. got. That is a difference of ablaut, between so-called e-grade vocalism and o-grade vocalism. But the (le-) in le-loip-a also exhibits what grammarians call reduplication: a morpheme that serves to show that we are talking about something that has happened (perfect tense) rather than something that is happening (present tense). The fact that the person doing the action was I (not he, she or they) is marked now by -a, not -o. This

is another morpheme that is used with the perfect tense. A simple past tense (I left) is e-lip-on. You can see clearly that there is in the core of this word not leip- or -loip-, but -lip-. This is called zero-grade vocalism. In Ancient Greek ablaut, you have a choice of e, o or nothing (called zero). The -i- is part of the underlying basic root of the word (lip) and does not take part in ablaut alternations. The prefix e- is a morpheme indicating the past tense, and -on is now the third morpheme we have seen that indicates that the person doing the action is I.

Declensions

The French singer Jacques Brel made Latin declensions famous in his song "Rosa", in which he goes through the forms rosa, rosa, rosam, rosae, rosae, rosa, rosae, rosae, rosas, rosarum, rosis, rosis. These are all the forms that can be taken by the basic word rosa, meaning rose. But what are they all for, except torturing generations of schoolchildren?

When learning Latin, there is no getting around the need to memorize declensions.

What Makes Up a Language?

The purpose of these endings is to indicate the different grammatical roles that the word can play in any utterance. This is perhaps most easily shown in a table:

ROSA	nominative	Indicates the subject of the sentence, e.g. *The rose is beautiful*
ROSA	vocative	Indicates the addressee, e.g. *O rose, thou art fragrant*
ROSAM	accusative	Indicates the object, e.g. *She plucked the rose*
ROSAE	genitive	Indicates possession, e.g. *The petals of the rose are yellow*
ROSAE	dative	Indicates that the action is done *for* the noun: *He bought some fertilizer for the rose*
ROSA	ablative	Indicates that the action is done by or with the noun: *She killed the prince with a rose dipped in poison*

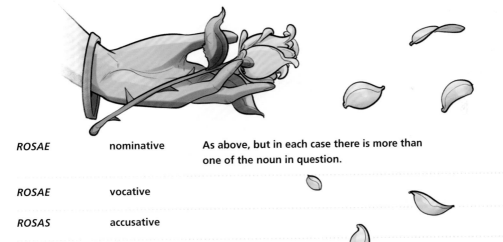

ROSAE	nominative	As above, but in each case there is more than one of the noun in question.
ROSAE	vocative	
ROSAS	accusative	
ROSARUM	genitive	
ROSIS	dative	
ROSIS	ablative	

The languages of the world can be described as either isolating or synthetic, depending on their morpheme-to-word ratio.

What is immediately apparent in the table on page 39 is that there is some ambiguity in this system. The word *rosae* by itself could be any one of four cases. You have to rely on the context to make the meaning clear.

There is nothing like the system of Latin declensions in Italian. But take the word *donne*: you cannot tell its morphological form just by looking at it. It could be the singular of a word like *amore*, whose plural is *amori*. Or it could be the plural of a word whose singular is *donna*. The latter is actually the case, so Italian is called a word-and-paradigm language (like Latin, Greek and many others). There might be all sorts of endings, but they are not unique in meaning and you cannot always reliably tell the grammatical category of a word merely by looking at its endings. This is very different from Turkish, in which each morpheme has just one meaning.

Morphemes in different languages

We have seen that words in English, French, Latin, Ancient Greek and German may be made up of several morphemes. The morpheme-to-word ratio of a language is an indicator of the kind of language that it is. In Classical Chinese, the ratio is 1:1. Sentences are composed entirely of free morphemes. A language that behaves like this is called an isolating language. Languages with a higher morpheme-to-word ratio are called synthetic, and these are further divided into inflecting (or fusional) and agglutinative languages.

An inflecting language uses one bound morpheme to encode a number of grammatical facts all at the same time. Thus in French, *donnai* can only mean *I gave*: but the facts that the action was past not present, active not passive, first person singular and indicative are all encoded in the suffix *-ai*. The sequence *-ai*, however, is also found in other forms, for example the future *donnerai* (*I shall give*). It is present in its root form in *j'ai* (*I have*). Latin *salvo* means *I save*: the ending *-o* tells you that this is first person, singular, present, indicative and active. But the Latin morpheme *-o* has other uses: it can indicate the dative or ablative masculine singular of some nouns and adjectives. Thus *salvo* could also mean *for the safe man*.

An agglutinative language is quite different. It makes meaning from strings of bound morphemes that have one, and only one, use. Turkish and

What Makes Up a Language?

"That which is alike will be called same. That which is not same is different."

Leonard Bloomfield

Japanese are classic example of agglutinative languages. In Turkish you can tack onto a basic word a string of bound morphemes that always have the same meaning wherever they are found: *oyma* (*sculpture*), *oyma-cı* (*sculptor*), *oyma-cı-lar* (*sculptors*), *oyma-cı-lar-ım* (*my sculptors*), *oyma-cı-lar-ım-ız* (*our sculptors*), *oyma-cı-lar-ım-ız-dan* (*from our sculptors*).

Languages as different as English and Chinese have one thing in common: they have little or no inflection, so word order is very important. Whereas English says *three dogs*, Chinese just strings together the words for *three* and *dog* and does not feel any need to alter the latter to show plurality. In neither language could you say *dog three*; word order rules would not allow this. In Latin you can vary word order: because of the endings, there is no ambiguity whether you say *tres canes* or *canes tres*. In French, you might say *Jean tira sur le pianiste* ("John shot the pianist") but to say *Le pianiste tira sur Jean* would be quite the opposite. In Ancient Greek, you can reverse the order of subject and object and still have the same meaning: *basileus eide doulon* and *doulon eide basileus* both mean "a king saw a slave".

Unlike English, Chinese does not alter the word for *dog* to indicate there is more than one, but in both languages, the number of dogs must come first. In Latin, the word order can vary.

Lexicon

A *lexeme* is the fundamental form of a word – the most basic version, without any prefixes or suffixes or other related grammatical variations. A *lexicon* is the sum total of *lexemes* in a language.

If you open a dictionary, you will find that the words that are defined are generally in bold type, whereas the definitions are in ordinary type. People who make dictionaries are called lexicographers; the words they print in bold and for which they provide definitions are called headwords.

Lexemes

You saw in an earlier chapter (see Morphology, page 34) that a word can be a tricky thing to define, and may be very different from language to language in terms of the number of underlying ideas that it encodes. The word is a tricky concept in lexicography too. If we take German *Maus*, *Mäuse* (*mouse, mice*), is that one word or two? Most people would say that *Maus* is the basic word

and *Mäuse* is just the plural, so that the headword ought to be *Maus* and we do not expect a separate dictionary entry for *Mäuse*. What about Spanish *soy (I am)*, *son (they are)*, *era (I was)*? Should there be three separate headwords? In fact, they are normally grouped under the infinitive form *ser (to be)*. In the same way French *je suis*, *ils sont* and *j'étais* are grouped together under *être (to be)* and English *be*, *are* and *was* would usually be grouped together under *be*.

This means that the total number of headwords in a language is far less than the total number of possible words found in text or speech. Linguists call these headwords lexemes. Just as a phoneme is a minimal unit of sound that distinguishes one word from another (English *pin*, *bin*, see Phonology,

Maus, Mäuse

From a lexicographer's point of view, it doesn't matter how many German mice there are – only the single *Maus* gets a headword.

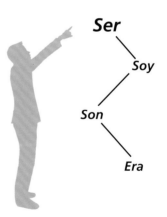

Ser

Soy

Son

Era

There is little point in looking for the words *soy, son* and *era (I am, they are* and *I was)* in a Spanish dictionary: they are all grouped under *ser*, the verb *to be* in its infinitive form.

What Makes Up a Language?

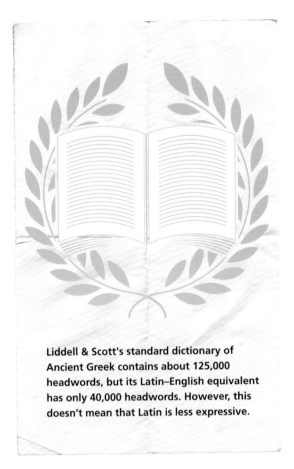

Liddell & Scott's standard dictionary of Ancient Greek contains about 125,000 headwords, but its Latin–English equivalent has only 40,000 headwords. However, this doesn't mean that Latin is less expressive.

The standard dictionary of the Welsh language, *Geiriadur Prifysgol Cymru*, runs to four volumes and has 105,586 headwords.

page 28) and a morpheme is a minimal component of meaning (Italian *do*, *diamo*, see Morphology, page 36), so a lexeme is the basic unit of meaning in terms of individual concepts that can be strung together to make larger statements. Lexemes are conventionally written in small capital letters. So the English words *give*, *gave*, *given* are all parts of the lexeme GIVE, and the German equivalents *gib*, *gab*, *gegeben* are all parts of the lexeme GEBEN. The total set of lexemes within a given language is referred to as its lexicon.

How many words are there in a language?

From time to time you come across little quizzes on the Internet designed to test your vocabulary in your native language. These quizzes test whether you know the meanings of words that become progressively more obscure as they go along. If you know, say, 100 really obscure words, the algorithm behind the program extrapolates the conclusion that you probably have a vocabulary of around 40,000 words.

This prompts the more interesting question of how many lexemes there are altogether in any one given language. There is no sensible way to answer this because there is nobody to keep count. The nearest you can get is to ask how many headwords there are in, for example, the *Oxford English Dictionary*. There are about 600,000 separate vocabulary items in this dictionary. You could try the same kind of thing with French, German, Arabic, Chinese, Japanese or any other language: find a really large dictionary from a reputable publisher and count the headwords. Although a dictionary can never be the last

In every language, there are words with more than one meaning. As Cicero noted in the 1st century BC, there could never be enough Latin words for all things to be given their own specific terms.

word in defining how many words there are in a language, it does give a general idea. If you look, for example, in the standard dictionary of Ancient Greek compiled by Liddell & Scott, you will find about 125,000 headwords. Some of these are very rare compounds, such as *ekekheirios*, which means "marked by a cessation of public business" (apparently found twice in inscriptions and used of sporting events). The standard Welsh dictionary, *Geiriadur Prifysgol Cymru*, runs to four volumes and has 105,586 headwords. In the *Oxford Latin Dictionary* you will find just 40,000 headwords.

Does this mean that Latin is a less expressive language than English or Greek, mired in a sort of lexical poverty? It does not. More than 2,000 years ago the Roman orator and lawyer Cicero mused on this problem and concluded *non verborum tanta copia est res ut omnes propriis vocabulis nominentur*: "there is not a sufficient supply of words for all things to be named with their own specific terms". He was talking about Latin, but it is true for all languages. There are far more thoughts

and ideas in the world than you could ever assign individual labels to. All languages make some words do at least double duty. For example, Latin *manus* usually means *hand*, but it can also mean *band* in the sense of a group of armed men. Greek *krino* basically means *to separate* but can also mean *to judge* because judging involves teasing apart (that is to say, separating) things that often look quite similar. In French, *la manche* can mean *sleeve* but it can also denote the English Channel or any other watery strait. Irish *lasc* etymologically means a *lash* or *whip*, but can also refer to the switch on a light or radio. So there are more senses in a language than there are headwords in the dictionary.

This is important because it is easy to make the mistake of thinking that a given language is somehow limited because it has a smallish lexicon. That would be as silly as supposing that a language with a smaller number of inflections is less expressive than one that has a lot. Apart from -*s* and -*d* in some verbs (*like*, *likes*, *liked*) and some tricky plurals (*men*, *teeth*, *mice*), English

What Makes Up a Language?

is practically devoid of inflectional morphology. Sanskrit, by contrast, has 24 forms for most nouns and far more for verbs. And yet speakers of English do not typically feel unable to express themselves; they just do it using different tools. What is true of morphology is also true for the lexicon. The fact that Latin has a smaller recorded vocabulary than Greek does not mean that speakers of Latin were restricted in the number of ideas in their heads.

New words

Languages do acquire lexical items from outside their original sources, however, whether by conquest, trade or the activities of intellectuals. The Germanic element in English was boosted by a lot of words that came from Norman French. Thus, alongside Germanic *ox*, to signify a living bovine quadruped, there is the word *beef*, which denotes only the meat of the animal once it is dead. In French, *boeuf* can be used both of the living animal and its meat. In England after the Norman Conquest, the French terms were hived off for culinary purposes, among others; this was doubtless a reflection of the dietary preferences and speech habits of the new Norman ruling class. The same is true for *pig* and *pork*.

Apart from straight borrowings like this, there is also the so-called calque. One type is where a new word is coined by taking a foreign one and translating it, lexeme for lexeme, into the target language. French *gratte-ciel* (literally *scratch-sky*) is calqued from US English *skyscraper*. English *scapegoat* is an interestingly colourful calque resulting from early misunderstanding of the Hebrew Azazel, probably the name of a demonic entity thought to live in the wilderness. The translators of the Hebrew Bible into Greek (in the 3rd century bc) took it as *ēz-'ozēl* ("goat that goes away") and gave it the Greek rendering

Semantic calque

The English word *scapegoat*, like the French *bouc émissaire*, is based on a literal translation from the Greek that was itself a translation – or rather mistranslation – of a word found in the Hebrew Bible, which the ancient Greeks took to mean "the goat that goes away".

apopompaios ("the one that is sent away"). Later English translators produced *scapegoat*, and French ones *bouc émissaire*. Both cases are examples of a semantic calque, which tries to get across the idea of the goat that is sent away to take with it the sins of the people.

Syntax

Syntax is to language what the rules of the road are to driving: it tells you about the order in which things happen.

Phonetics and phonology describe how sounds are made and combined into larger units; morphology describes how larger units are combined or modified to create different meanings. Syntax looks at how words are combined to create a larger entity: the sentence.

Grammatical "rules"

At a banal level, syntax can be about no more than making sure that sentences are grammatical, in other words that they conform to the "rules" of the language. If we ask where these rules come from, there is no straightforward answer. But speakers of any language tend to observe certain fundamental rules, even if they differ over more subtle matters. Thus in French, for example, it is

Sticking to the rules

Every language has its own set of fundamental rules, and some of the more subtle ones can be particularly difficult for non-native speakers to get right.

not permissible to say *je chez rentré suis moi*; word order requires that you say *je suis rentré chez moi*. Likewise in English you can say *I went back to my house* but not *my back I house to went*. No speaker of these languages would violate these rules (unless for some deliberate effect) because they are so fundamental.

There are more subtle rules that not everyone gets right. Most people do not say in French *si je vous verrai demain, je vous donnerai un cadeau* (literally "if I will see you tomorrow, I will give you a present") because future stems are prohibited in clauses that begin with *si*. The correct French would be *si je vous vois demain* ("if I see you tomorrow"). But, probably because of a mistaken analogy with a separate construction known as the logical future (for example, *quand je vous verrai, je vous donnerai un cadeau*; literally "when I will see you, I will give you a present"), it is happening more and more. It is likely that an increasing number of speakers will soon not perceive it as incorrect at all.

Speakers of English nowadays typically ignore subjunctive forms and modal verbs: instead of *If I were in charge, I should not permit it* most people say *If I was in charge, I would not permit it*. Most people understand what is being said. The difference between French and English is that France has the Académie Française, which acts as a watchdog of the language. It publishes prescriptive grammars and dictionaries. People can ignore these, but there is in theory somewhere to look if you want definitive rulings on these matters. In English there is the *Oxford English Dictionary* for words and spelling, but no comparable authority for syntax. That said, French people going about their everyday lives do not have a strong sense of

What Makes Up a Language?

the existence of any centralized linguistic authority; of those who do, few would worry about such academic questions in ordinary colloquial speech as opposed to careful writing.

The problem with prescriptiveness in language is that any attempt to freeze the language at some chosen point is bound to fail. Language is not a static phenomenon and is constantly changing. Some people will regret the loss of an expressiveness that they valued in this or that word or construction but change is irresistible, even if it moves at a different pace among different groups within a population. The generally unexpressed view on the street seems to be that anything goes, as long as you are not misunderstood.

Ambiguity and phrase structure

Questions of ambiguity are of interest to students of syntax. Imagine that a spy is sent this message: *You must get some more convincing evidence.* Does this mean that the evidence already gathered

Established in 1635, the Académie Française in Paris has the last word on the usage, grammar and vocabulary of the French language.

is convincing, but that more is needed? Or does it mean that the existing evidence is not convincing enough and that the spy must be more critical about the quality of the material she sends back? It could be rather important. One can neatly indicate the problem by bracketing: it is a difference between *more* (*convincing evidence*) and (*more convincing*) *evidence*.

The concept of bracketing can be applied more widely and systematically to the structure of sentences in general, in which case it is known as phrase structure grammar. Thus the sentence *Une femme française étudie le roman russe* ("A French woman studies the Russian novel") could be analysed first into subject (*une femme française*) and then predicate (*étudie le roman russe*). The predicate is simply that which is said of the subject.

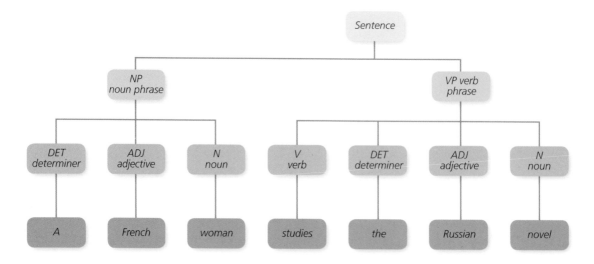

But you can go deeper than this, as can be seen from the diagram above.

From a functional perspective, you could substitute for the noun phrase (NP) *Une femme française* ("a French woman") another NP, such as *Le scientifique bulgare qui vient tout juste de consommer un peu trop rapidement son petit déjeuner insolite de muesli et de lait de coco et qui commence à ressentir les symptômes fâcheux de la maladie de reflux gastro-oesophagien* ("The Bulgarian scientist who has only just eaten his unfamiliar breakfast of muesli and coconut milk rather too quickly and is beginning to suffer the unwelcome symptoms of gastro-oesophageal reflux disease.") The sentence would still make perfect sense, the two NPs being functionally identical units in spite of their difference in content and the greater length and complexity of the second NP.

This approach is particularly useful if you are trying to learn a foreign language. It makes you focus on the meaningful units of which utterances are composed and helps you to manipulate them so as to produce new sentences. Consider the sentence in Spanish *el político mintió muy convincentemente* ("the politician lied very convincingly"). The last two words are adverbs, which are units that modify a verb. *Convincentemente* describes the manner in which the politician lied, and *muy* indicates the degree to

which *convincentemente* applies. Taken together, these two words form a single adverbial phrase. You could in principle replace it with another adverbial phrase, such as *en la rueda de prensa* ("at the press conference") or *ayer por la mañana* ("yesterday morning"). The first is an adverbial phrase of place and the second one of time. You could not replace this unit with any noun phrase, though, such as *el electorado cansado* ("the weary electorate"). You cannot say *X mintió Y*; you have to say *X mintió a Y*. This is because *mentir* (to lie) is an intransitive verb and so cannot take a direct object; it has to take a preposition like *a* (*to*). But you could replace the adverbial phrase with an

When learning a foreign language, it can be helpful to focus on meaningful units and phrases that can be grouped together to form new sentences.

What Makes Up a Language?

adverbial clause of result, for example *con el fin de obtener un resultado favorable en las urnas* ("in order to ensure a favourable outcome at the polls"). That clause looks different from *muy convincentemente*, but is a functionally equivalent unit: it describes how the politician lied.

Grammars of this kind are useful to people who are learning a new language. But they also have their limitations: they do not tell you how to produce new sentences. They rely on the learner sensing similarities between different kinds of structure and knowing what can be substituted or expanded. This is where transformational generative grammar comes to the fore – it seeks to provide algorithmic instructions like lines of computer code so as to generate grammatical sentences from first principles.

Transformational grammar

Transformational grammar may be credited to the American linguist Noam Chomsky (b. 1928) whose book *Syntactic Structures* (1957) marked the beginning of the astonishing modern dominance of syntax in the field of linguistics. Chomsky has reformulated his theories over the last 60 years. They are of intense interest to specialists in computer translation, but his original motives for investigating this field had nothing to do with computers.

The chief interest of transformational grammarians has always been with the question of how language works in the brain. Although we refer to *learning* languages, linguists tend to reserve that term for what we do with foreign languages; to describe how infants pick up

Noam Chomsky's syntactic structures

Noam Chomsky is perhaps the most famous linguist of the 20th century. He attempted to use almost mathematical formalisms to explain the underlying structures in the human brain that process language and are responsible for filtering out impossible utterances.

How language works in the brain

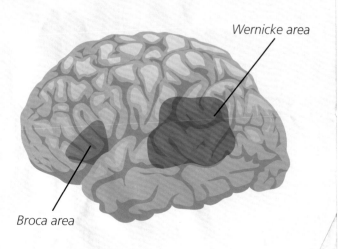

Wernicke area

The Broca area is the part of the brain responsible for speech production, while Wernicke's plays a key role in the comprehension. Damage to either area can lead to speech and language problems. For example, a person with Wernicke's aphasia has trouble understanding spoken or written words, but can still speak fluently, even if what he says makes little sense.

Broca area

their native language they tend to use the word *acquisition*. This is because they take the view that rules are subconsciously absorbed in such contexts without formal instruction. Chomsky's original idea was that there are deep structures that pass through transformations and are finally realized in speech or writing as surface structures. These transformations look rather like mathematical functions acting on a set: they tell you how to arrange a sequence of words and morphemes in order to generate a new sentence.

Consider the affirmative *Hans hat das Buch gekauft* ("Hans has bought the book") and the interrogative *Hat Hans das Buch gekauft?* ("Has Hans bought the book?"). To turn a statement like this into a question, the standard grammars tell you to invert the auxiliary verb (*hat*) and its subject (*Hans*). That is satisfyingly simple. But a transformational grammarian might want to write:

NOUN PHRASE1 + AUXILIARYHABEN +
NOUN PHRASE2 + VERBPAST PARTICIPLE
⇨ AUXILIARYHABEN + NOUN PHRASE1 +
NOUN PHRASE2 + VERBPAST PARTICIPLE

To get from the active *Hans hat das Buch gekauft* to the passive *Das Buch wurde von Hans gekauft* ("the book was bought by Hans"), the traditional approach will tell you to put the thing that is suffering the action (*das Buch*) first, add the correct form of the auxiliary verb *werden*, then add the word *von* and the name of the agent (*Hans*) and finally add the past participle of the main verb. It is surprisingly easy to teach this to students with only a few examples from which they readily assimilate the pattern. A transformation, on the other hand, might look like this:

NOUN PHRASE1 + AUXILIARYHABEN +
NOUN PHRASE2 + VERBPAST PARTICIPLE
⇨ NOUN PHRASE2 + PAST AUXILIARYWERDEN +
von + NOUN PHRASE1 + VERBPAST PARTICIPLE

The second case is more complex because, in reality, one needs other transformations to show how to conjugate the auxiliary verb; explaining how to form the past participle is likewise tricky in terms of linear algorithms. Some facts of language are just given: it is hard to describe in purely computational terms why *werden* inflects as it does and why not all past participles are as regular as *gekauft*.

What Makes Up a Language?

Transformations may look like an attempt at higher algebra, and it is true that many linguists are really basically mathematicians. They are in search of ever more elegant theoretical formalisms in which to clothe their perceptions. In the real world, you have to search quite hard for language textbooks that make use of algebraic transformations – not least because they are even more off-putting than the traditional terminology.

But in what sense might these transformations really exist? Are they hard-wired into the neural architecture of the brain? Presumably not: a boy born in New York to Japanese parents will not be able to speak Japanese unless he hears people around him speaking it. But if transformations are not part of neurology (or hardware, to use a computing analogy) they might nevertheless be part of psychology (or software, to use the same analogy).

Without assuming the existence of something of the kind, say proponents of transformational grammar, it is hard to see how speakers differentiate quickly and reliably between grammatical and ungrammatical structures. It is unlikely that we all have in our heads billions of possible forms, some labelled as grammatical and some as the opposite. Some simpler rules must exist, even though these too must still be very numerous and complex. But if humans are programmed to manipulate linguistic components, why do English children produce mistaken forms like *goed, *thinked, *sticked, *sheeps? This cannot be the result of imitating adults. If it is a fault with their initial software, where do they get the upgrade that turns them into grammatically mature adults?

Language is not innate: a boy born in New York to Japanese parents will only learn to speak Japanese if he regularly hears it being spoken.

Language Families

The Holy Roman Emperor Charles V said that to know another language was to possess another soul. The more you look at other languages, the more you are struck by their diversity. Like travel, exposure to other languages broadens the mind: you become aware that different groups make use of quite different inventories of sounds. The !Xoo language, spoken by some 4,000 people in Botswana and Namibia, has about 40 consonant phonemes of the kind made while breathing out. In addition, it has around 80 sorts of click made by creating a closure in the mouth while breathing in. English, by contrast, has only 24 consonantal phonemes.

When travelling, we come to realize how different the structures of other languages can be. Learners of French and German are used to a system of tenses in their verbs, indicating when a thing happened. But some languages have fewer tenses, or more, or different ones, or none at all. Vocabulary is also an eye-opener: English and French *cousin*, for example, are thought sufficiently clear for speakers of those languages. But many cultures would be amazed that no distinction is made between sister's child and brother's child.

Indo-European Languages

The Indo-European language family probably had its origins somewhere in the Russian steppes thousands of years ago.

Have you ever been to a foreign country and recognized words in the local language in spite of never having studied it? An English speaker might see a connection between German *Licht* and English *light*. Not only do Hindi *pitā* and Icelandic *faðir* mean the same thing (*father*), they have grown from the same root. How can this be?

The "lost source"

The awareness that languages have similarities, not only in individual words but also in the ways that

their grammars operate, is not new. In 1786, the lawyer and linguist Sir William Jones made a speech before the Asiatic Society of Bengal about Sanskrit, the ancient classical language of India (which has a status similar to that of Latin in Europe). He said that it was "more perfect than the Greek, more copious than the Latin, and more exquisitely refined than either, yet bearing to both of them a stronger affinity, both in the roots of verbs and the forms of grammar, than could possibly have been produced by accident; so strong indeed, that no philologer

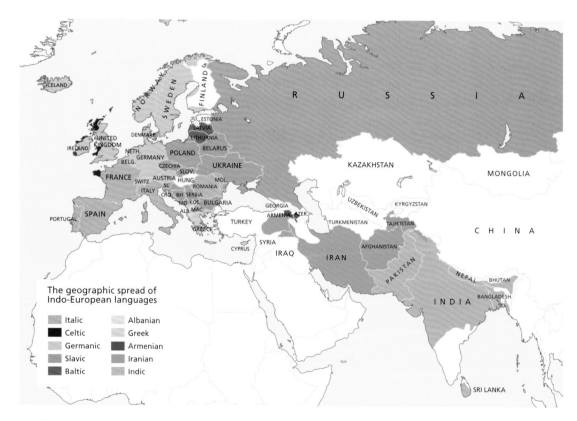

The geographic spread of
Indo-European languages

- Italic
- Celtic
- Germanic
- Slavic
- Baltic
- Albanian
- Greek
- Armenian
- Iranian
- Indic

Language Families

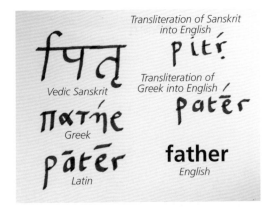

Jacob Grimm's law explains how languages that are seemingly unalike can derive from the same lost common ancestor by tracing correspondences between them. For example, the initial *p* found in Sanskrit, Greek and Latin versions of the word for *father* shifts into *f* farther down the line in Germanic languages such as English.

could examine them all three, without believing them to have sprung from some common source which perhaps no longer exists". Jones is nowadays perhaps the person most closely associated with this discovery. But the Dutch scholar Marcus Zuerius Boxhorn, a professor at Leiden, had as early as 1647 posited a genetic link between Sanskrit, Latin, Greek, Celtic and Iranian languages. The French Jesuit Gaston-Laurent Coeurdoux had published similar ideas in 1767.

This hypothetical lost source is what pioneers such as Franz Bopp, Rasmus Rask and Jacob Grimm went on to investigate more thoroughly in the following century. They did this by looking beyond the obvious correspondences into the deeper structures. *Licht* and *light* are easy. But what about English *father* and German *Vater*? Jacob Grimm formulated regular laws of sound change that explained how these forms had evolved from a common ancestor, which they thought was likely to have been **pater*, which can be confirmed by looking at Sanskrit *pitar*, Greek *pater* and Latin *pater*. Going even deeper, we might consider items such as Latin *-fendo* and Greek *theino*. Both

Jacob Grimm (1785–1863) devoted his life to literary research. In his pioneering *Deutsche Grammatik* (1819–37), he traced the development of the Germanic languages for the first time.

The development of the Indo-European proto-language

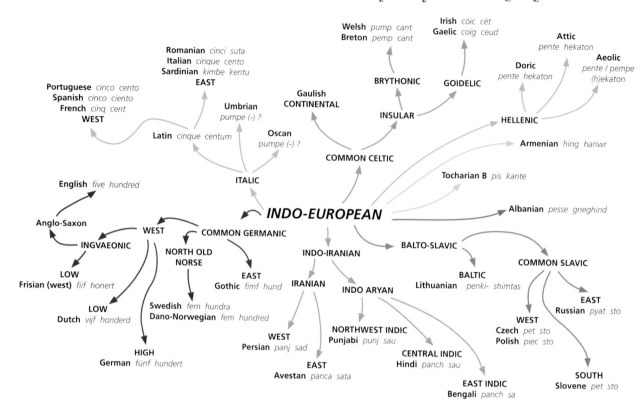

mean *to hit*. But are they related? Yes: although f- and th- might seem some way apart, the parallel correspondence between Latin *formus* (hot) and Greek *thermos* show that there is a pattern. It seems that there must have been an earlier element that regularly evolved into Latin *f-* and Greek *th-*: it is conventionally represented as **gwh-*.

Those asterisks are used to mark reconstructions. What is being reconstructed is what linguists nowadays call Indo-European. Boxhorn called it Scythian (for historical reasons that need not detain us here) and German-speaking scholars often still call it *Indogermanisch*. It is the hypothetical, lost common ancestor of Latin, Greek, Sanskrit, Armenian, Welsh, Irish, Old Church Slavonic and Gothic in much the same way that Latin (which is neither hypothetical nor lost) is the ancestor of Romance languages such as French, Italian, Spanish, Portuguese and Romanian. The map on page 54 shows just how widespread the Indo-European languages are. They are spoken from India in the east to Iceland in the west.

Comparative philology

This grouping of languages into families based on similarities of vocabulary and grammatical structure is the task of comparative philology. Words for common things such as parts of the body, family members, plants and animals are helpful starting points. You can see from the spider diagram above that numerals are also especially revealing. Greek *pente*, Welsh *pump*, Sanskrit *pancha* and Avestan *panca* (five) can be shown to derive regularly from Indo-European **penkwe-*. Latin is odd in that it has *quinque*. The weight of evidence among the earliest-attested languages suggests that *p-* was original and that Latin did something new by changing it to *qu-*, apparently under the

Language Families

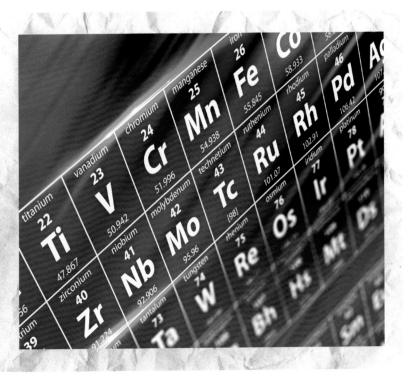

A number of elements of the periodic table have names with roots in Latin, such as Caesium (from *caesius*, meaning *sky blue*) or Greek, such as Lithium (from *lithos*, meaning *stone*).

influence of -*que* at the end of the word. French *cinq* and Italian *cinque* evolved later from this Latin innovation. Gothic *fimf* and German *fünf* can be accounted for by the same kind of sound change that links German *Vater* and Latin *pater*. Where Indo-European has initial **p-*, Latin and Greek will also generally have *p-*, but the Germanic languages will have an *f-* sound.

The word for *hundred* is likewise revealing. The Indo-European was **kmtom-*. It is not hard to connect this with Latin *centum*. Greek *hekaton* requires a little more historical work, but is definitely related. Sanskrit *shatam* and Lithuanian *shimtas* are perhaps a surprise, however. Dialectologists once thought that, if you drew a line from Kaliningrad on the Baltic to Odessa on the Black Sea, you would find that in all languages west of that line the initial **k-* evolved into hard *c-*

(centum languages) whereas to the east it became *s-* or *sh-* (satem languages). The discovery in the 20th century that Tocharian, a very long way to the east in Chinese Turkestan, is actually a centum language ruined this neat dialectal theory. It continues to puzzle those who seek to understand early population movements.

The scientifically minded reader would not be mistaken to see a link between the activities of comparative philologists since the 19th century and the classification of plants into families by Carl Linnaeus, of animals into species by Charles Darwin and of elements into the periodic table by Dmitri Mendeleev. In the next two sections, you will look more closely at the intellectual basis for classifying languages into families and the question of whether all likenesses are to be accounted for simply in terms of lineal descent.

Other Language Families

Of the 7,000 or so languages spoken in the world today, the vast majority are not Indo-European. Do they also belong together in families, and do they share any common ancestry?

Classifying languages

There are basically three ways to classify languages: geographically, typologically and genetically. The geographical approach is helpful for anthropologists and others who are interested in what is to be found "on the ground" in a particular location. But if you ask what languages are spoken in Nigeria, for example, the answer is more than 500. If somebody says that the "national" language is English, that is a political statement, not a linguistic one. The geographical approach is interesting for what it tells us about population movements and the growth of the nation-state. But if you want to look at the matter like a linguist, you will want to group languages together on the basis of shared features, as for the Indo-European family.

One way of thinking about shared features is by means of typology, which looks at things such as word order. For example, Hindi and Japanese and Latin are all SOV (subject-object-verb) languages, in which the *subject* of a sentence tends to precede the *object*, with the *verb* coming last. English, by contrast, is a SVO language: the subject first, then the verb, then the object. Arabic and Hebrew are VSO languages: verb first and then the rest. Such correspondences are genuinely interesting, but it is not clear whether the similarity between Hindi and Japanese word order is any more than coincidental.

In Nigeria, more than 500 different languages are spoken, including Igbo, Hausa and Yoruba.

English is an SVO language: the subject comes first, followed by the verb and the object. In Latin, the verb tends to appear at the end (SOV), while in Arabic, sentences start with the verb (VSO).

Language families and the genetic method

The most widespread and popular method of language classification has tended to be the genetic method. This looks at similarities and differences between languages to establish a sort of family tree. The relationships have traditionally been detected by comparing shared items of vocabulary, but a more nuanced approach can also make use of typological features such as phonology, morphology and syntax. The more features that are common to a set of languages, the more justification there is in putting them together into one family.

For example, Turkish is spoken in Turkey; Uyghur is spoken in the Xinjiang Uyghur Autonomous Region in the far northwest of China; Dolgan is spoken by about 1,000 people in the far north-east of Siberia. These are just three members of the Turkic group, which contains several dozen

Turkish, Uyghur and Dolgan, spoken in Turkey, north-west China and northeast Siberia respectively, are all members of the Turkic group of languages.

Word	Azerbaijani	Kazakh	Kyrgyz	Turkish	Uyghur	Uzbek
Mother	*ana*	*ana*	*ene*	*anne*	*ana*	*ona*
Father	*ata*	*äke / ata*	*ata*	*baba*	*dada / ata*	*ota*
One	*bir*	*bir*	*bir*	*bir*	*bir*	*bir*
Two	*iki*	*yeki*	*eki*	*iki*	*ikki*	*ikki*

related languages. These languages are not unified by geography; indeed, they are widely dispersed across areas of the globe and exist in close proximity to unrelated forms of speech such as Arabic, Persian, Russian and Mongolian. But the genetic relationship between them is pretty clear if we take a look at some items of vocabulary (see box above for examples).

The cladistic method

There is an obvious parallel between the way that linguists group languages together on the basis of shared features and the way that biologists do the same with organisms.

All living things can be grouped together at various levels of generality, starting from a kingdom (e.g. animals as opposed to plants), then progressing through phylum (e.g. chordates), class (e.g. mammals), order (e.g. primates), family (e.g. hominids), genus (e.g. *homo*), species (e.g. *Homo sapiens*). This process is called cladistics, from the Ancient Greek word *klados*, meaning *branch*, and the individual branches are called clades.

The desire to categorize living things or the chemical elements or languages or religions or any other phenomenon in this way is a product of the Enlightenment and the compilation of the great *Encyclopédie* by Denis Diderot (1751–72).

Although there is a parallel between what scientists and linguists do in this respect, it is not a perfect one. In order to classify organisms into a tree, for example, one needs to have descent from a common ancestor. That requires some degree of historical record, which might range from fossils that are millions of years old to stuffed specimens

put in a museum by Victorians. Every time some new characteristic appears, a branch is added to the tree.

The diagram below shows the clades for organisms descending from an original type that we may call A. It does not matter what kind of organism it is. In this situation, B and C differ from A and from each other, but they have enough of the characteristics of A that you can safely say that they come from A and not something else. D and E both have a great deal in common with B, but they differ from it and from each other. D and E stand to B just as B and C stand to A; each pair exhibits innovations with respect to a common ancestor and each member of the pair has innovated differently. F shows progressive innovation with respect to C; it differs from C but has more in

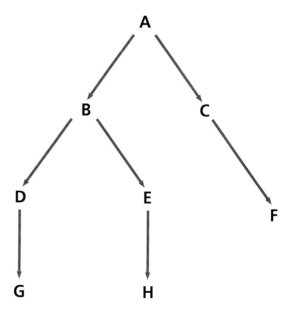

the past and know how people were speaking. In particular, even if the so-called Out of Africa theory of human evolution is correct (see Human Evolution, page 17), so that all modern human beings have one single shared origin, we cannot suppose that the earliest humans started speaking one language at a time when they were all together as one group. It is quite possible that early humans separated into groups before they developed articulate language and that they then arrived at different forms of speech independently of each other.

In that case, even if human beings have one shared origin, we would be dealing with polygenesis as far as language is concerned. If you can find enough continuous historical evidence, it might well be possible to draw up a tree of the kind that biologists use to say, for example, that Vedic (an ancient language of India that has its origins in the middle of the 2nd millennium BC) and Homeric Greek are more like each other than either is like Arabic, with the result that Vedic and Greek ought to be grouped together and separately from Arabic. But Vedic

Between 1747 and 1772, Denis Diderot oversaw the publication of 28 volumes of his *Encyclopédie*, a "Classified Dictionary of Sciences, Arts and Trades".

common with C than with B, D or E. Finally, G is obviously the descendant of D because it is like it but different, and H is the descendant of E for the same reasons. D, E, G and H have more in common with each other and with B than any of them does with C or F.

In search of the ancestors of language

Life scientists often work with the hypothesis of monogenesis, meaning that a given organism is taken to have had one, and only one, origin: the sexual or asexual reproduction of its parent(s). In languages, we cannot assume at a theoretical level that all observed languages descend from one common ancestor. We simply do not have the ability to see tens of thousands of years into

The form of Greek used by Homer in the *Odyssey*, the opening lines of which are shown above, has its roots in the very earliest stages of the Greek language.

Linguists have little hope of ever finding written records of Indo-European, the lost ancestor of Latin, Greek and Sanskrit, among others.

and Greek, for all their similarities, are still very different from one another. They cannot sensibly be grouped together any more closely than G and F in the diagram on page 60.

But why say G and F? Why not simply call Vedic B and Greek C? Vedic has a lot in common with an ancient Iranian language called Avestan. Those two languages are more closely related to each other than either of them is to Greek, even though both Vedic and Avestan are to some extent like Greek. But Vedic and Avestan differ markedly in terms of their phonology.

Linguists assume that Indo-European (A) originally split into a number of groups: one was Indo-Iranian (B), the common ancestor of the Indian and Iranian languages, and another was Hellenic (C), the ancestor of the various Greek dialects. Indo-Iranian must have been a unity for a while, but then split into separate Indic (D) and Iranian (E) branches. Attic Greek (F) is one of several descendants of the Hellenic branch, while Sanskrit (G) and Avestan (H) represent further independent developments from their common ancestor.

The difference between linguistics and zoology

is that the only languages for which we have direct evidence are F, G and H. All the rest is reconstruction, a hypothesis to account for the later ramifications of the model. Palaeontologists, on the other hand, have fossils on which to base their judgments. With languages, nobody seriously expects to find written records of Indo-European or Indo-Iranian; with palaeontology, by contrast, there is always the hope that some physical piece of evidence will turn up to confirm or disprove this or that hypothesis.

Classification difficulties

Another thing to bear in mind is that the genetic method relies on the linguistic equivalent of mutation in animals. As you will see in the Romance languages chapter (see page 66), languages change over time because a group of speakers innovates in some way, but this is not the only way in which change can occur. As well as evolution over time there is areal diffusion, whereby speakers change their habits not by random mutation but because they come into contact with speakers of other languages through trade, marriage or war. Whereas

> ## "A speaker is like a lousy auto mechanic. Every time he fixes something in the language, he screws up something else."
> *Joseph Greenberg*

in biology animals of a different species cannot breed with each other, there is no such restriction in language, so a simple view of genetic descent will always fall short of complete accuracy. In terms of the diagram on page 60, it is as though H, although quite independent of F, acquired some features of it by direct contact.

The cladistic method works best when there is some time depth to the data to which it is applied. The Indo-European languages are a good example of this, and scholars have been working on them for a long time. If you look at the languages of Africa, however, the picture is very different. Interest in Africa took some time to progress beyond colonial exploitation; serious linguistic study cannot be said to predate the last quarter of the 19th century and much of the work of classification came as late as the pioneering publications of American anthropologist and linguist Joseph Greenberg in the 1950s.

Greenberg's work was controversial and has since been refined by critical debate, but this only serves to underline the difficulty in reaching agreement in a field in which there are thousands of varied languages to study, indigenous written records do not reach very far back and external interest began only quite recently.

As a result, some linguists say that there is no point trying to group languages into phylum, class, order, family, genus and species; the most one can do is to group together into families (using the term in a different, wider sense) those that seem to belong together, and accept that some families will have hundreds of members whereas others might have only two or three. There is also the problem of isolates (solitary languages with no known relations), the most familiar of which is probably Basque. This is a somewhat despairing view; as we have seen in the case of Indo-European, it is quite possible to establish a carefully differentiated family tree.

Basque, also called Euskara, is not related to Indo-European languages such as French and Spanish.

Macro-families

Some linguists argue that you can classify the more than 7,000 languages of the world into just 18 different family groups

Phylum	Some examples
Afro-Asiatic	Arabic, Ge'ez, Hausa, Hebrew, Somali
Altaic	Japanese, Korean, Mongolian, Turkish
Amerindian	Cherokee, Cree, Nahuatl, Zapotec
Australian	Jarrakan, Wunambal
Austro-Asiatic	Khmer, Mon, Vietnamese
Chukotko-Kamchatkan	Chukchi, Kamchadal/Itelmen
Dravidian	Brahui, Kannada, Malayalam, Tamil, Telugu
Eskimo-Aleut	Aleut, Inuit, Yupik
Indo-European	Greek, Sanskrit, Hindi, Armenian, French, German, English
Kartvelian	Georgian, Laz, Mingrelian, Svan
Khoisan	Khoe, Nossob
Na-Dene	Navajo, Tlingit
Niger-Congo	Igbo, Shona, Swahili, Wolof, Xhosa, Yoruba, Zulu
Nilo-Saharan	Luo, Kanuri, Songhay
Sino-Tibetan	Burmese, Cantonese, Mandarin, Min, Tibetan, Wu
Tai-Kadai	Lao, Thai, Zhuang
Trans-New-Guinea	Engan, Mek, Teberan
Uralic	Estonian, Finnish, Hungarian, Saami

Macro-families

An interesting problem occurs if, instead of looking at differentiation, you run the process backward and look at the largest possible groupings that you can find. If you try to classify language families into something like what zoologists call phyla, how many such macro-families might you have? Some linguists would argue for as few as 18 (see above).

The problem with such a view is this: if you can whittle down more than 7,000 languages into only 18 macro-families, why stop there? What is it that tells you that you have reached the boundary of one class and that it is genetically distinct from another? It might be generally agreed that the vocabulary and typological features of, say, Afro-Asiatic and Indo-European are so different that they must be separate entities. But attempts have been made to explain away these differences. Look at the following data:

Phylum	Form	Meaning
Nilo-Saharan	*tek	one
Indo-European	*deik-	to point
Amerindian	*tik	finger
Sino-Tibetan	*tik	one

At first glance, this kind of demonstration is very beguiling. We see some similarities of sound and meaning and suppose that these four enormous language groups have a common ancestor. But there is a problem. To say that the Amerindian word for *finger* is tik involves taking a very crude "average" across hundreds of different languages. The word for finger in Quechua, a member of the Amerindian family, is *pallqa* or *ruk'ana*, so it is hard to see how *tik can stand for the entire family.

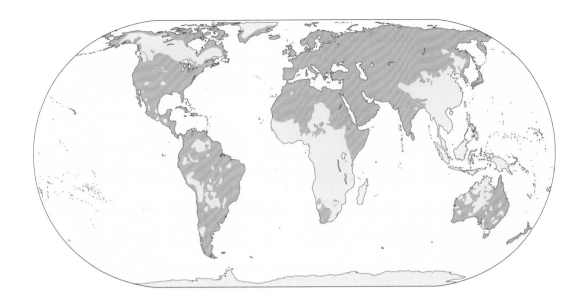

The Dravidian word is *birelu*, which is left out of the discussion of this particular etymology for obvious reasons, although Dravidian words are pressed into service in other cases when they fit the pattern better. Proponents of such connections are forced to propose ever more unlikely correspondences supported by less and less plausible processes of sound change. And the correspondences are also problematic at the semantic level. Why should *finger*, *one* and *point* once have been a unitary concept? There is no more necessary link between those words than between, say, *finger*, *five* and *wave*.

Advocates of the approach believe in a super-macro-family called Nostratic, the supposed ancestor of several already hypothetical macro-families – see the diagram below.

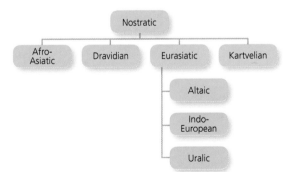

This map shows the distribution of the hypothetical Nostratic family of languages. The name is derived from Latin *nostrates*, meaning *fellow countrymen*.

As advanced nowadays, the hypothesis does not seek to explain every macro-family. The maximal distribution can be seen from the map above. It is striking that even so bold an approach stops short of trying to integrate the languages of sub-Saharan Africa and China.

There are nevertheless those who would pile speculation upon supposition and extrapolate backward from Nostratic to an entity called Proto-Human, surely the most ambitious mega-family imaginable. This would be the progenitor of all languages spoken on Earth. It is like trying to reconstruct the original speech of humanity before the confounding of tongues described in the biblical story of the Tower of Babel. It is hard to imagine a time and place where there could have been an actual community of speakers of Proto-Nostratic. Furthermore, if the Out of Africa theory is correct, it is surprising that the Niger-Congo languages have no part to play in Proto-Nostratic.

Romance Languages

From the 3rd century BC onward, the influence of Rome extended steadily through Italy and then over the Alps into the rest of Europe, down into Africa and across into Asia. Countless people came to use Latin in areas where it was previously unknown.

Latin was not just one variety of speech, any more than English is. There was an elite form that we find in the works of writers such as Virgil and Cicero, but spoken Latin must have varied according to the status (actual or aspirational) of speakers, their educational attainments and their geographical location. This is the same everywhere.

Everyday Latin

Many surviving inscriptions and graffiti differ from elite usage, giving us an insight into the language of ordinary people. But even literary sources cast some light on this. The comic writer Plautus (254–184 BC) uses features that look colloquial compared with other writers. Instead of the usual *parvus* and *magnus* for *small* and *big*, Plautus often uses *minutus* and *grandis*. This is particularly significant if we bear in mind that the French, Italian and Spanish for *big* are *grand*, *grande* and *grande* respectively. The normal word for *horse* in literary Latin is *equus*, but Horace uses *caballus* pejoratively to mean *nag*. Once again it is noteworthy that the French,

Italian and Spanish for *horse* are *cheval*, *cavallo* and *caballo* respectively. Allowing for sound changes, you can see that these derive from a term that is not unknown in literary Latin, but which is marked as non-standard.

Such examples could be multiplied, but the ones given suffice to make the point. Just as Latin descends from Indo-European, so French, Italian, Spanish, Portuguese and others descend directly from Latin. We can say that they are more closely related to Latin than to any other language in the group because this particular evolutionary path was taken by speakers of Latin and not of Sanskrit, for example. The latter language went its own way and gave rise to Hindi, Bengali, Marathi and countless other Indian languages (which you will examine later).

Not all horses are equal: one Latin speaker's horse (*equus*) is another one's nag (*caballus*).

Language Families

The precise means by which this happened are controversial. In the 19th century, ideas of class, dignity and decadence made it natural to think in terms of Vulgar Latin, a form of sub-standard Latin that degenerated further to give the languages of today. Although that does not quite mesh with Victorian ideas of progress, it does fit with their romantic ideas about ancestors being somehow perfect and descendants a bit of a disappointment.

The Latin "reformers"

This narrative does not entirely lack corroboration. The so-called *Appendix Probi* is attributed to a teacher of Latin grammar named Probus who lived in the 3rd or 4th century AD. It is arranged in three columns: on the left, Probus gives the correct Latin form that he wants people (probably scribes) to use, in the middle and all the way down is the Latin word *non* (*not*) and on the right is the mistaken form that he wants people to avoid. Some examples are in this table:

"Correct" Latin	NOT	"Vulgar" Latin	Meaning
speculum	non	speclum	mirror
baculus	non	vaclus	stick
avus	non	aus	grandfather
miles	non	milex	soldier
equs	non	ecus	horse
favilla	non	faille	ash
formosus	non	formunsus	beautiful
nubes	non	nubs	cloud
aqua	non	acqua	water
glis	non	gliris	dormouse
numquam	non	numqua	never
vobiscum	non	voscum	with you

This is a short selection from a very much longer list. Reading it, you can almost hear the angry tone of a schoolmaster slamming his hand on the table, "No! Don't say X! Say Y! How many times must I tell you?"

Plainly, there must be some truth in the account of Latin changing and people trying to stop it. St Augustine in the 5th century AD felt that his Latin was purer than that of some of his contemporaries. Emperor Charlemagne in the 9th century AD felt

As well as Latin, the *lingua franca* of his empire, Charlemagne (AD 742–814) probably also spoke a Rhenish Franconian dialect of Old High German.

that the process had gone too far and tried to arrest it by prescribing standards of "proper" Latinity. The problem comes when change is necessarily characterized as decline. Many people want the world to be as it was at some idealized time in their own memory, and view any deviation as a matter for regret. But in truth all languages have been in a state of flux for as long as we can trace them. There is nothing unique about the way in which the Romance languages evolved from Latin. Hindi, Bengali, Marathi and Punjabi descend ultimately from Sanskrit via various Prakrit intermediaries. The various Iranian languages descend from Proto-Iranian in a similar way.

Alternative theories

Some writers have found the chief motor for the rise of the Romance languages in the barbarian invasions that caused the fall of the

No. 2740. Y. Checa. Invasion des Barbares. Y. Checa

Roman Empire in the 5th century AD. There is some justification for this; some structures of administration and cohesion inevitably broke down. But linguistic change within all varieties of Latin was not unknown before this cataclysm, and it is notoriously difficult to achieve consensus on the question of how long after the fall of Rome you have to look before finding a variety of language that is so undeniably different from Latin that it must be something else.

Complex phenomena that extend over time and space can rarely be explained by a single event, or even a process such as the disintegration of an empire and declining linguistic standards. Even at the height of Roman power, there must have been many spoken and written varieties of Latin within Italy and across the wider territories under the control of Rome. The influence of Rome is obviously important for explaining why it is that people were speaking a variety of Latin and not, say, Greek. But further than this one cannot go without giving simplistic explanations that will not stand up to scrutiny.

Alaric I and his Visigoth troops ransacked the city of Rome in AD 410, an event that marked the beginning of the end of the Roman Empire. According to some theories, this led to the rise of Romance languages.

It has been aptly pointed out that if we had Latin and French but no other languages in the Romance family, you would not be able to tell whether the two were parent and child or daughters of the same lost ancestor. Just because one language (French) appears to have evolved more than another (Latin), it does not follow that the former evolved *from* the latter. They might just be children that have developed at different rates and in different ways. Once you line up Italian, Spanish and Romanian, however, you see at once that they are more like each other than they are like Latin. Their shared characteristics point to common innovations during their descent over time from the same parent. In addition, you cannot say that if one variety of speech differs from another by more than a certain percentage, then you have a different language.

Language Families

What counts as a new language?

Imagine that it is the year AD 1300 and you take a long walk from southern Italy to northern France. The varieties of speech that you hear at the beginning and end of your journey will be very different. But as you go from village to village, the differences will sound much more gradual. The same must be true for linguistic change over time. It undeniably happens, but it is not really possible for later linguists to say, "Aha! Now, for sure, we have a new language." As much as anything, it matters what the speakers themselves say about their varieties of speech. Although it has long been traditional for scholars point to parts of the Strasbourg Oaths of AD 842 as the earliest example of French, there is no evidence that the participants

Only 10,000 of us speak Mirandese

The rest of us speak Portuguese!

Portugal

The Strasbourg Oaths, a pledge of allegiance between the rulers of East and West Francia signed in AD 842, were long said to contain the earliest examples of written French.

thought of this language as French. The words *François* or *Roman* are not used to describe the language before about AD 1020.

The varieties of Romance language

Romance languages did not spread across all areas of Roman influence. They took hold chiefly in western Europe: the areas that today we call France, Spain, Portugal, Italy, Romania. But there are many varieties. Linguists do not quite agree on how many Romance languages there are, not least because of the often unhelpful distinction that is made between languages and dialects. The table on page 70 gives an idea of their variety, geographical extent and numbers of speakers.

If you have never heard of Ligurian, you are in good company. Remember that there are more than 7,000 languages spoken in the world today and most of us have not heard of even a fraction of them. But if you think that Mirandese, spoken by only 10,000 people, cannot be a real language at all because of its small number of speakers, you might want to have a look at the section of this book that deals with dialects (see page 162).

Romance languages spoken in Europe

Language	Number of speakers in Europe (rounded)	Where spoken in Europe
French	63,000,000	France, Switzerland
Italian	58,000,000	Italy, Switzerland
Spanish	38,500,000	Spain, Gibraltar
Romanian	20,000,000	Romania, Moldova
Portuguese	10,500,000	Portugal
Napoletano-Calabrese	5,700,000	Italy
Sicilian	4,700,000	Sicily
Catalan	4,000,000	Spain, Andorra, France
Venetian	3,800,000	Italy
Lombard	3,600,000	Italy
Galician	2,500,000	Spain
Sardinian	1,200,000	Sardinia
Piedmontese	700,000	Italy
Picard	500,000	France
Ligurian	500,000	Italy
Friulian	300,000	Italy
Extremaduran	200,000	Spain
Arpitan	150,000	France, Italy, Switzerland
Corsican	125,000	Corsica
Occitan	110,000	France
Asturian	100,000	Spain
Aromanian	50,000	Greece, Romania
Jèrriais	45,000	Channel Islands
Romansch	40,000	Switzerland
Aragonese	30,000	Spain
Mirandese	10,000	Portugal
Fala	6,000	Spain
Minderico	500	Spain

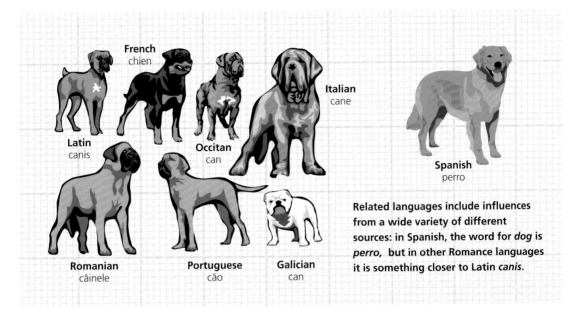

French
chien

Italian
cane

Latin
canis

Occitan
can

Spanish
perro

Romanian
câinele

Portuguese
cão

Galician
can

Related languages include influences from a wide variety of different sources: in Spanish, the word for _dog_ is _perro_, but in other Romance languages it is something closer to Latin _canis_.

The varieties of Romance language have a great deal in common, however, especially in terms of lexicon and morphology. Why is _perro_ the Spanish word for _dog_ when in the other languages it is something closer to Latin _canis_? The origin of _perro_ is uncertain – it is most probably derived from an unrelated language, such as that of the Iberians who inhabited the peninsula before speakers of Indo-European arrived. It is an important reminder that languages are made up of things from all sorts of sources, and that you cannot simply apply a uniform algebraic transformation to turn Latin neatly into one of its daughter languages.

Grammar is also very similar across the Romance group. If we look at the irregular verb _to be_, we find the following correspondences:

	Latin	**French**	**Italian**	**Spanish**
_I am_	_sum_	_suis_	_sono_	_soy_
You are	_es_	_es_	_sei_	_eres_
He, she, it is	_est_	_est_	_è_	_es_
We are	_sumus_	_sommes_	_siamo_	_somos_
You are	_estis_	_êtes_	_siete_	_sois_
They are	_sunt_	_sont_	_sono_	_son_

You can immediately see that French is closest to Latin in the forms – the first sound in _êtes_, for example, is just what happens when an /s/ drops out from the inherited Latin form and affects the pronunciation of the preceding vowel. There are regular sound laws (see pages 55 and 74) that show a similar kind of thing happening elsewhere:

asinus ⇨ ***asine*** ⇨ **asne** ⇨ **âne**
Latin **Old French** **Modern French**

It is the mixture of the regular and predictable with the irregular and unpredictable that gives the characteristic shape to each of the Romance languages. Why are Latin and Italian different? Part of the reason is simply because of independent innovations over time among speakers, which also account for why Indian languages are like, but different from, Iranian ones. We might call these vertical (or diachronic) factors. But there are also horizontal (or synchronic) factors: borrowings from speakers of other languages, either in a territory newly conquered or by trade and social dealings. These are called areal influences.

Germanic Languages

The Germanic languages belong to the Indo-European family. It is hard to say precisely when speakers of Germanic languages split off from the other Indo-European peoples and established themselves elsewhere.

Germanic tribes, around AD 100

- North Germanic
- Ingvaeonic
- Istvaeonic
- Irminonic
- East Germanic

On the basis of archaeology, it seems that North Germanic peoples had settled by 1200 BC in southern Sweden, Denmark and Schleswig-Holstein. Around 700 BC, East Germanic tribes split off and moved east toward the Vistula. Already by the 3rd century BC, distinct West Germanic tribes were to be found across the Netherlands and northern Belgium. Around AD 100, the Roman historian Tacitus describes these West Germanic tribes as subdivided into three groups: the Ingvaeones, Istvaeones and Irminones (see map above).

The major Germanic languages in current use are English, German, Dutch, Danish, Norwegian, Swedish, Icelandic, Faroese, Frisian, Yiddish, Pennsylvania Dutch and Afrikaans. Yiddish is a special case; it was once spoken by around 10 million people in Germany, Poland and central Europe. Although more German than anything

else, it is not straightforwardly a Germanic language, being a complex mixture of German, Slavonic and Semitic elements. It is first attested around the 12th century AD and is written in the characteristic square alphabet of Hebrew.

All of the Germanic languages are related to each other, of course, and can be arranged in a tree (see opposite above). The picture on the ground is a good deal less tidy. New High German is simply the technical name for standard modern German, spoken throughout Germany and parts of Switzerland. But there are many other varieties of New High German that linguists classify as languages rather than dialects (see Dialects, page 162). The table opposite gives some examples.

New Low German describes a number of varieties of German spoken in northern Germany and the eastern part of the Netherlands.

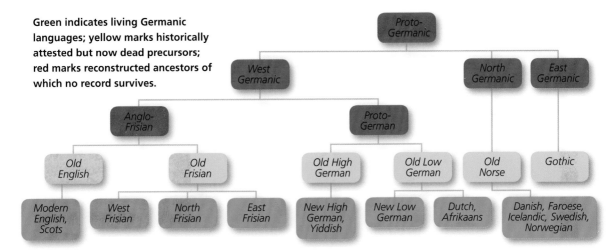

Green indicates living Germanic languages; yellow marks historically attested but now dead precursors; red marks reconstructed ancestors of which no record survives.

Proto-Germanic

West Germanic — North Germanic — East Germanic

Anglo-Frisian — Proto-German

Old English — Old Frisian — Old High German — Old Low German — Old Norse — Gothic

Modern English, Scots — West Frisian — North Frisian — East Frisian — New High German, Yiddish — New Low German — Dutch, Afrikaans — Danish, Faroese, Icelandic, Swedish, Norwegian

Changing sound patterns of Germanic languages

In terms of sound, all the Germanic languages underwent a number of significant and characteristic changes that differentiate them very clearly from the rest of the Indo-European family. They are known collectively as the First Germanic Sound-Shift (or Grimm's Law, after its discoverer Jacob Grimm, the philologist also known for publishing *Grimm's Fairy Tales* with his brother Wilhelm, see page 55) and can be seen quite readily if you look at some vocabulary (see table on page 74).

What is usually called Grimm's Law is in fact a series of three separate changes of sound. By Grimm I, the voiceless stops become voiceless fricatives; by Grimm II, the voiced stops become voiceless; by Grimm III, the voiced aspirates become voiced stops. For a reminder about the terminology, see Voice and Speech, pages 20–22, and Phonology, page 28.

But people soon noticed some puzzling irregularities. If an original *p* is supposed to become an *f*, why do we have, for example, modern German *sieben* (*seven*), with a voiced stop, in contrast with the Latin *septem*?

The Danish linguist Karl Verner spotted the reason. Where an original Indo-European *p*, *t* or *k* appears in the middle of a word and the preceding syllable is not stressed, Grimm I is not the final stage: a further evolution resulted in a voiced consonant.

You can see this most clearly with two kinship terms. In Indo-European *bhráter* (*brother*), the accent is on the first syllable. This is paralleled in

Language	Number of speakers	Place
Palatinate Franconian	400,000	Rheinland-Palatinate
Ripuarian	250,000	North Rhine-Westphalia
Upper Saxon	2,000,000	Dresden, Leipzig, Saxony-Anhalt
Swabian	820,000	Baden-Württemberg
Cimbrian	3,000	Trent, Verona, Vicenza
Móchena	2,000	Trent, Verona, Vicenza
Lower Silesian	12,000	Silesia (Poland)

Sound	Latin/*Indo-European root	Gothic	English	Sound Law
p	**p**ater	fā**ð**ar	**f**ather	**Grimm I**
t	**t**urba	**þ**aúrp	-**th**orp	
k	**c**aput	**h**aubiþ	**h**ead	
b	*dheu**b**	diu**p**s	dee**p**	**Grimm II**
d	**d**ecem	**t**aihun	**t**en	
g	**g**enu	**k**niu	**k**nee	
bh	*bher-	**b**aíran	**b**ear	**Grimm III**
dh	*dheig-	**d**aigs	**d**ough	
gh	*we**gh**-	gawi**g**an	cf. wa**g**on	

Sanskrit *bhrát-*. Old English *brōþor* has the sound that we expect to correspond to this (þ, called "thorn", is a voiceless fricative, as in English *thin*). Indo-European *patér*, on the other hand, has the accent on its last syllable. Sanskrit *pitár* corresponds. The voiced stop in Old English *faeder* is the result of the operation of Verner's Law. So when the accent *precedes* the consonant in question, it remains voiceless; when the accent *follows*, the consonant becomes voiced.

A trace of this can be seen in English *éx-it* beside *ex-ís-ted*. The former has the accent on the first syllable; many speakers pronounce the /x/ unvoiced as *ék-sit*. The latter has the accent on the second syllable; it is not accidental that many speakers pronounce the /x/ with voice, as *eg-sís-ted*.

Germanic word order

Many people who learn German are very soon struck by what seems to them to be its peculiar word order. Look at this sentence: *Heute glauben wir daß diese Politik gefährlich ist* (literally, "today believe we that this policy dangerous is"). Why say *believe we* rather than *we believe*, and why *dangerous is* rather than *is dangerous*? If we were not careful, we might think we were listening to Yoda in the *Star Wars* films ("When nine hundred years old you reach, look as good you will not.").

So far as it can be reconstructed from the earliest sources, such as Vedic, Hittite, Homeric Greek and early Latin, the Indo-European parent of the Germanic tongues appears originally to have been a SOV (subject-object-verb) language – in other words, one where the subject of the sentence comes first, then the object and finally the verb (see Syntax, page 46). *Homo canem videt* ("the man sees the dog") is the natural word order in Latin even if others are permitted (because, in an inflected language, little if any ambiguity would result from rearranging the words).

The German Indo-Europeanist Jakob Wackernagel pointed out in 1892 that certain elements in a sentence could appear in the second place in

Simultaneous translators have a tricky job working from German, as the verb appears at the end of a subordinate clause – they have to wait for it before they can start translating.

Language Families

The only times a verb appears at the start of a sentence in modern German are in questions, commands or conditions.

various languages in the group. These elements lacked an accent and are called enclitics. In particular, Wackernagel noted that the verb in main clauses in Sanskrit is unaccented. So there seems to have been at least a tendency quite early in Indo-European for the verb to migrate toward the beginning of its clause. This gradual "lurch to the left" was so marked that we find in early runic texts, before AD 600, ordinary declarative main clauses in which the verb stands first. So the German verb has had a remarkably mobile history.

In modern German the most usual word orders are SVO (subject-verb-object), SVA (subject-verb-adverbial phrase or clause), AVS (adverbial clause-verb-subject) or, mainly in poetry, OVS (object-verb-subject). The verb does not come first except in questions, commands or conditions. The tendency is, in fact, for it to stand as the second element in a main clause. This explains why, in the example

above, we have *heute glauben wir*: because the adverb *heute* comes first, the verb will regularly follow and its subject must come third. If the sentence began *Wir glauben* with no adverbials, the verb would still be in second position.

One explanation for the verb standing last in the subordinate clause (*daß diese Politik gefährlich ist*) might be that German has conservatively preserved the Indo-European tendency to put the verb last. But the historical evidence says otherwise. There was no preference for verb-final dependent clauses until, in the 16th century, they became standard practice in chancery documents from Nuremberg. By the 18th century, school grammars were prescribing this as normal. Whether this is due to the influence of a scribal elite that knew and was imitating Latin is controversial. People who work as simultaneous interpreters will tell you that this makes it particularly hard to interpret from German into English or French or Italian because you get to a certain point in the sentence and then have to wait to find out what the verb is going to be.

Celtic Languages

The Greek historian Herodotus, writing in the 5th century BC, mentions *Keltoi* living by the River Danube near modern Herbertingen in southern Germany.

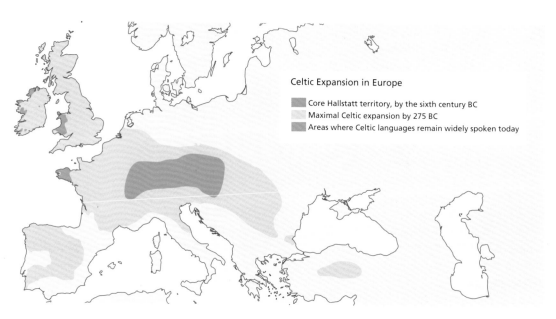

Celtic Expansion in Europe

Core Hallstatt territory, by the sixth century BC
Maximal Celtic expansion by 275 BC
Areas where Celtic languages remain widely spoken today

Celts are associated with two major phases of the European Iron Age: the Hallstatt culture (8th to 6th centuries BC) and the La Tène culture (6th to 2nd centuries BC). It is not clear when they separated off from other Indo-Europeans. They were found in Spain, France and Germany, across Central Europe into Anatolia, up into Britain and Ireland and down to northern Italy. They were dominant in the British Isles by about 250 BC, and until the invasions of Julius Caesar.

Varieties of Celtic

Celtic is the name for the group of languages spoken by Celts. Some people use the terms Continental Celtic and Insular Celtic to distinguish between the varieties found on mainland Europe and Britain respectively. This can be confusing; Breton, spoken in Brittany, is classified as Insular because its early speakers migrated from Britain. Examples of Continental Celtic were Gaulish, Lepontic and Celtiberian. Gaulish was spoken by Gauls, whose territories covered all of modern France, some of Switzerland, northern Italy and parts of Hungary. Lepontic is attested by inscriptions found in northern Italy, while Celtiberian is also known from inscriptions found in northeastern Spain. All members of the Continental group were extinct by about AD 600.

Linguists also commonly make a distinction between P-Celtic and Q-Celtic. This reflects the fact that in the Brythonic Celtic group (see table opposite) the inherited Indo-European labiovelar *kw developed into a labial /p/, whereas in the Goidelic group it became a velar /k/ (which for historical reasons is referred to by the letter Q), as in the modern Irish *cam*, meaning *bent*.

For example, the Indo-European for *five* was **kwenkwe*. In Welsh, which belongs to the Brythonic (P-Celtic) group, the two labiovelars became labial /p/, so that the Welsh for *five* is *pump*. In Old Irish, which is a Goidelic language, the labiovelars became velar /k/ (spelled with a *c*), so that the Old Irish for *five* is *cóic*.

The Indo-European for *horse* was **ekwos*. The name of the Gaulish horse-goddess Epona appears to derive from this, and the presence of /p/ for inherited /kw/ suggests that Gaulish was also P-Celtic. So the P/Q distinction does not map neatly onto the Insular/Continental divide.

The same can be seen with the word for *four*:

Only six Celtic languages survive, which are all of the Insular type. They may be classified as shown in the table to the right.

There are relics of other Celtic varieties in Britain, for example Cumbric, used chiefly in Cumbria, with variants as far away as Yorkshire. The so-called Cumbric Score is a method of counting sheep still used in some parts of the North of England. The following correspondences between the variety of Cumbric found in Swaledale (there are many others) show how close the numbers sometimes are to Welsh:

Numeral	Swaledale Cumbric	Welsh
1	yan	un
2	tan	dau
3	tether	tri
4	mether	pedwar
5	pip	pump
10	dick	deg
15	bumfit	pymtheg
20	jiggot	ungain

Insular Celtic

P-Celtic Brythonic			Q-Celtic Goidelic		
Northern	Southern		Western	Eastern	
Welsh	Cornish	Breton	Irish	Manx	Scots Gaelic

Mutation in Insular Celtic

One of the most striking things about the sound system of the Insular Celtic languages is the phenomenon of mutation. This causes consonants at the beginning of a word to change depending on the context in which the word is used.

To take just Welsh, for example, the dictionary form of the word for cat is *cath*, but it can appear as *gath* (lenition), *ngath* (nasalization) or *chath* (aspiration). All four forms have the same lexical meaning but they differ in sound and spelling. In part, this is the sort of phenomenon that exists in other languages (in Sanskrit it is most fully worked out) and is called sandhi. But there is also a grammatical element to it:

ei gath	fy ngath	ei chath
his cat	my cat	her cat

You can see that *his* cat is *gath* whereas *her* cat is *chath*, even though the preceding word is *ei* in both cases. So mutation is not just about phonetics; it is also about grammar. Whatever its origins, mutation makes it very hard to look words up: you will not find *ngath* in a typical Welsh dictionary. The compilers assume that users know the rules!

Slavonic Languages

Like the Romance languages, the Slavonic languages are members of the larger Indo-European family, but they also belong together as a distinct subgroup.

Whereas the common ancestor of the Romance languages survives in the form of Latin, we no longer have direct evidence of Proto-Slavonic, the forerunner of the Slavonic languages. Linguists have to reconstruct it by extrapolating backward from the evidence of existing Slavonic (and other Indo-European) languages.

The earliest attested Slavonic language is called Old Church Slavonic. The texts are biblical and liturgical, mostly translated from Greek as part of the spread of Christianity into Slavic territories. The earliest manuscripts date from the 10th or 11th century AD but preserve material dating from the late 800s AD. They are written in the distinctive Glagolitic script. This is rather different from the modern Russian alphabet, which is known as Cyrillic because it is attributed to St Cyril. Some modern Slavonic languages are nowadays written in the Roman script (for example Czech, and Polish).

The Slavonic group is modest in size in terms of the number of languages spoken, but very large in terms of the number of speakers, who are found over much of central and eastern Europe. The language with the largest number of speakers (138,000,000) is Russian. Ukrainian is spoken by about 33,000,000 people and Polish by about 39,000,000. The remaining languages, although of great cultural significance, have fewer than 10,000,000 speakers each. Their distribution is shown on the map below.

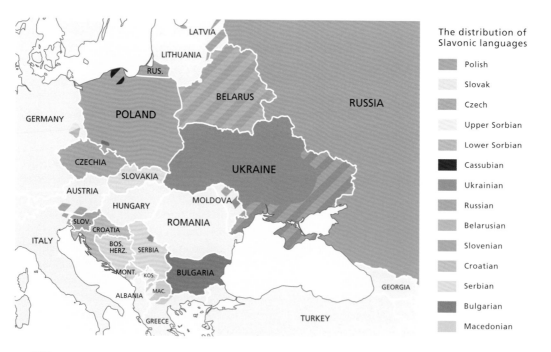

The distribution of Slavonic languages

- Polish
- Slovak
- Czech
- Upper Sorbian
- Lower Sorbian
- Cassubian
- Ukrainian
- Russian
- Belarusian
- Slovenian
- Croatian
- Serbian
- Bulgarian
- Macedonian

Language Families

The family of Slavonic languages has comparatively few members, but numbers more than 220 million speakers across central and eastern Europe.

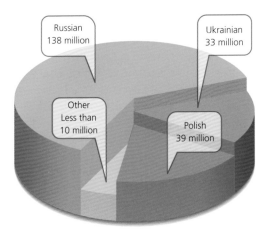

Russian
138 million

Ukrainian
33 million

Other
Less than
10 million

Polish
39 million

Palatalization of Slavonic languages

Perhaps the most striking audible surface feature of the Slavonic languages when compared with the rest of the Indo-European family is the extensive palatalization that they have undergone. This means essentially that a stop or fricative sound is modified during its articulation by the middle portion of the tongue being simultaneously arched up toward the hard palate. Take, for example, the dental stop [t] in Russian: it exists, but there is also a palatalized variant written phonetically as [tʸ], the palatal element being indicated here by a superscript y. The difference can be heard if you think of English *too* beside *tube*. In the second case, there is a gliding effect after the [t]. You could contrast in the same way French *anneau* (*ring*; unpalatalized) with *agneau* (*lamb*; palatalized).

For each labial (*p, b, f, v, m*) and each dental (*t, d, s, z, n*) in Russian there is a phonemically distinct palatalized equivalent. This means that you get minimal pairs (see Phonology, page 29) of words that differ only according to whether there is palatalization. For example *brat* (*brother*) vs. *bratʸ* (*to take*), *mat* (*checkmate*) vs. *matʸ* (*mother*). The palatal glide at the end of the word is brief but audible; it is not a distinct sound, as in English *catty*.

Palatalization

A notable characteristic that separates the Slavonic languages from others in the Indo-European family is the extensive palatalization that affected them.

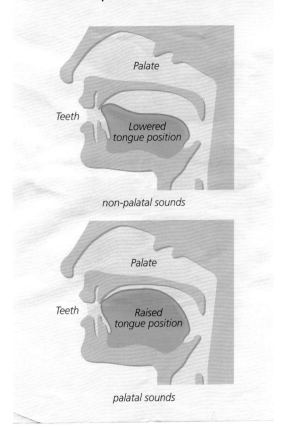

Palate

Teeth

Lowered tongue position

non-palatal sounds

Palate

Teeth

Raised tongue position

palatal sounds

Stresses and inflections

Another marked feature of Russian is the way that stress affects the quality of vowels in words. Although this is not unique to Russian, it is widespread and typical. Thus a word like *golova* (meaning *head*, and represented as gəlʌva in IPA) is not pronounced as spelled. The stress is on the last syllable. The result is that the apparent o-vowel of the first syllable is reduced to a short central a-vowel (as in the German *bekommen*, meaning *get*); the second o-vowel is reduced to a similar sort of [a] but with the tongue slightly lower. This phenomenon is called *akane* in Russian. Russian

Russian verbs are more subtle than most. Each one comes as a contrasting pair, to describe how events happened in time, rather than just when. For example, the perfective or bounded past describes a single event – "I wrote ten letters." The imperfective or unbounded past describes an incomplete or repeated action – "I wrote letters every day."

words are not written with accents, except in books for children. This means that a learner must know the accent on every word in order to be able to pronounce it correctly.

Slavonic languages are for the most part highly inflected, that is to say they use a wide range of prefixes, infixes and suffixes to mark different grammatical meanings. Bulgarian and Macedonian have lost most of the cases that are reconstructed for Proto-Slavonic and are still to be seen in Old Church Slavonic. But Russian, Ukrainian, Belarusian, Sorbian, Slovak, Slovene, Czech, Cassubian and Polish have six or seven cases for nouns. This means that these languages are quite conservative in terms of structure.

Aspects and tenses in Russian

Although English, French, Spanish, Italian and Hebrew, along with many other languages, have lost almost all of their cases over time, achieving many of the same results by a combination of word order and prepositions, not all languages have done the same thing.

The Russian verb is extremely subtle in several ways. Part of the complexity lies in its system of so-called aspects. Most people are familiar with tenses, which locate the action of a verb relative to a particular timeframe. Thus French *je donnai* (*I gave*) happened in the past and *je donnerai* (*I shall give*) refers to the future. But what about *je donnais* (*I was giving*)? Is just as much a past event as *je donnai*. The two differ not in respect of *when* they happened but *how* they happened. It is their intrinsic extension over time that is being described. *Je donnai* describes an action that is bounded, over and done with; *je donnais* describes an action about whose completion no comment is made. Maybe the action was abandoned before being finished. This bounded aspect is called perfective and the unbounded is the imperfective.

In Russian, this way of looking at things is pervasive. Every verb in Russian comes as one of a pair that contains contrasting perfective and imperfective members. This distinction cuts across tenses and moods and extends to forms such as the infinitive (to *X*) and participle (*Xing*).

The perfective past indicates a single event: for example, *ya pazvanil* [perfective] *i skazal* [perfective] *n'et* ("I telephoned and said no"), whereas the imperfective past represents an incomplete action or one repeated; for example, *ya zvanil* [imperfective] *kazhdiy d'en* ("I telephoned every day").

The imperfective present describes a simple continuing present, as in many other languages, such as *stroit* (*he is building*). But when the perfective form is combined with present-tense endings, the result is a perfective future: *po-stroit* (*he will build*). This is because you cannot have a completed action described in the present tense. Every time a Russian uses any verb, she has to think about all of this. Other languages can express these things, but they are not obliged to.

Russian verbs of motion

Verbs of motion are also famously tricky in Russian. In most languages, if you want to say that you are going to the bank, you use the neutral verb *to go*. In Russian you are faced with a battery of choices. First, you must choose between a pair of verbs, with one pair meaning "to go on foot" (*idti*; *khodit'*) and the other "to go by transport" (*ekhat'*; *ezdit'*). You must give this information; there is no neutral form that allows you to leave the matter unspecified. Then, from your chosen pair of verbs, you have to decide whether to use the first or second alternative.

The first alternative is used to describe travel in one direction at a particular moment; the second implies a return journey, or else movement in more than one direction. Thus if you meet someone in the street and ask where she is going you would

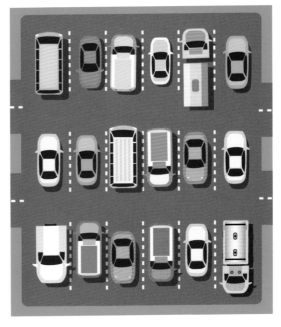

If you want to say you are going somewhere in Russian, the verb form you use depends on whether you will be walking or using a form of transport.

use part of *idti*; if a police officer stops a motorist and asks the same question, it would be part of *ekhat'*. By contrast, if you meet someone at home and ask if she ever takes a walk to the theatre, you would most likely use *khodit'* because you generally come home again after going to the theatre. If you say that when Mikhail lived in Leningrad he used to drive to work, you would use *ezdit'* because the usual thing is to drive home again afterward. In all, there are 14 common Russian verbs that behave in this confusing way.

Semitic Languages

The Semitic languages are part of a larger family called Afro-Asiatic, but it makes sense to discuss them as a subgroup because of their close similarities in terms of structure and vocabulary.

The best-known variety of Semitic, with the most speakers across the world, is undoubtedly Arabic, which has at least 350,000,000 speakers from Morocco to Iraq. The other living members of the family are Hebrew and Assyrian, the latter being the name given by its speakers to various modern varieties of Aramaic and Syriac. In the Horn of Africa are spoken Amharic (the modern successor to Ge'ez, or Ethiopic), Tigre and Tigrinya. In Malta there is Maltese. The distribution of the living languages can be seen from the map below. The group also contains a good number of older varieties that are either no longer found at all except in academic works (such as Akkadian, Epigraphic South Arabian, Ugaritic, Eblaite, Amorite, Moabite), or are preserved chiefly for religious purposes (Biblical Hebrew, Classical Aramaic and Classical Syriac).

The origins of Semitic languages

It is hard to understand the Semitic languages if you do not have some grasp of their history and interrelations, but their precise origins and diffusion remain a matter of lively debate. Some

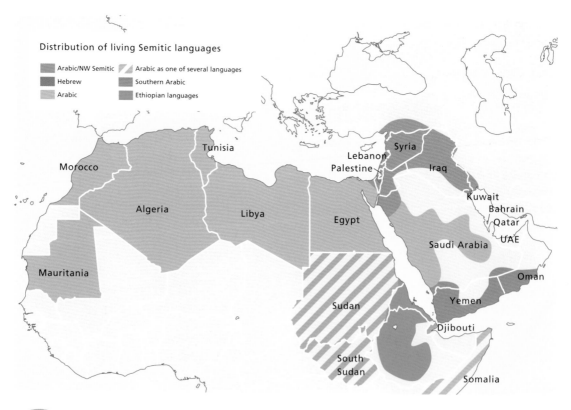

Distribution of living Semitic languages

- Arabic/NW Semitic
- Hebrew
- Arabic
- Arabic as one of several languages
- Southern Arabic
- Ethiopian languages

Morocco · Tunisia · Lebanon · Syria · Palestine · Iraq · Kuwait · Bahrain · Qatar · UAE · Algeria · Libya · Egypt · Saudi Arabia · Mauritania · Oman · Sudan · Yemen · Djibouti · South Sudan · Somalia

There is also the fact that Akkadian was for a long time the *lingua franca* of much of the Middle East, in the same way that Koine Greek was in the Mediterranean from about 300 BC to AD 600, and Latin was in medieval Europe. Akkadian in its various varieties (such as Babylonian and Assyrian) was widely used from about 1500 BC to about 500 BC.

After the Persians defeated the Assyrians, Imperial Aramaic (another Semitic language) enjoyed a fresh ascendancy as the language of government. So here too there are significant possibilities for the acquisition of traits by later influence, rather than inheritance. This state of affairs complicates or perhaps altogether defeats neat attempts at genetic classification. So, while these languages can be classified, any tree model is necessarily contentious.

Roots and patterns

One of the most striking features of all the Semitic languages is that they are root-and-pattern languages. Look at the following Arabic words:

kataba	he wrote
ya**kt**u**b**	he writes
u**kt**u**b**	write!
ki**t**aa**b**	book
ku**t**u**b**	books
kaa**t**i**b**	writer
ma**kt**a**b**	office
ma**kt**a**b**ah	library
ma**kt**u**b**	written

It is clear that the basic framework is K-T-B, and that all the other meanings are arrived at by rearranging the letters and inserting vowels according to a pattern that holds true across the language. Linguists call KTB the root of the word. It does not exist in any spoken sense because it cannot be pronounced, but it is in the brains of all

A bronze of Sargon, the king of Akkad. The Akkadian language was spoken in Mesopotamia from the 3rd to the 1st millennium BC.

think that the original homeland was the Levant (for these purposes, modern Israel and Syria), whereas others would place it more squarely in the Arabian peninsula. Whatever the true history of the population movements behind them, the Semitic languages can be arranged into smaller categories on the basis of shared features. The problem with this is how to present the results. Not many linguists are persuaded that the genetic tree model, which works quite well in Indo-European, is at all suitable for the Semitic languages. They were spoken in a much more confined area, so the possibility of areal influences (borrowing as a result of direct contact between neighbouring groups) is very real. To return to the genetic evolutionary metaphor, there might have been significant cross-fertilization between the various languages. Shared features of phonology, syntax or vocabulary could be the result of that kind of process, rather than direct inheritance.

speakers who know how to manipulate other such roots to create similar relationships.

The verb is a very striking part of the overall grammatical system of the Semitic languages. You have seen for the Slavonic languages how there is aspect as well as tense (see Slavonic Languages, page 80). In the Semitic languages, any verb may be inflected in a perfective or an imperfective form. The perfective conjugation is sometimes called the suffix conjugation because the personal endings are marked by suffixes: Arabic *katabtu*, *katabta*, *katabti*, *kataba*, *katabat* (*I wrote*, *you* (m.) *wrote*, *you* (f.) *wrote*, *he wrote*, *she wrote*). The imperfective is generally called the prefix conjugation, because it uses prefixes as well as suffixes: the corresponding forms of the Arabic verb *to write* are *aktubu*, *taktubu*, *taktubiina*, *yaktubu*, *taktubu*.

A page from a Hebrew prayer book known as the Rothschild Mahzor. This illuminated manuscript was made in Florence in 1490, and contains the full order of prayers for the year.

Broadly speaking, these do not indicate when a thing happened, but its extension over time. The perfective might conveniently be mapped onto the functions of a past tense, but that is because perfective actions naturally belong to the past. It can also be used to denote general truths (such as "Observers are agreed that …"). The imperfective, on the other hand, might represent a present or a future; the context, in particular adverbs of time or other markers, is critical for resolving ambiguities.

An Indo-European language like Latin has many tenses but only two voices (active and passive). Ancient Greek has more tenses and even an extra voice (the middle, which had various reflexive and intransitive functions). The Semitic languages have no real tenses, two aspects, but a considerable number of "derived" forms that are not quite like the voices of Latin and Greek, but can sometimes encode similar information.

For example, in Classical Hebrew the simple perfective verb *qatala* means *he killed*. But this can be modified to produce various other senses:

Grammatical form	Example	Translation
Kal	qatal	he killed
Niphal	niqtal	he was killed
Piel	qittel	he murdered
Pual	quttal	he was murdered
Hiphil	hiqtiil	he got X killed
Hophal	hoqtal	X got killed
Hithpael	hitqattel	he killed himself

You can see that Hebrew does by means of markers on the verb (grammaticalization) what English and other languages do by means of verbal circumlocutions (lexicalization). So in French you might say *Je me suis fait couper les cheveux* ("I got my hair cut") using a special construction with *se faire* followed by the infinitive; in Hebrew "to get something cut" is to cause it to be cut, so one could in principle simply put the verb *cut* into the Hiphil.

Language Families

Arabic has verb forms not found in other languages. Form IX is used only for verbs that express defects or colours, so, for example, to describe things – or people – turning red.

In Arabic, the verb has not seven but fifteen such forms. Some of these are not much used, or not at all for most verbs. The equivalent in Arabic of the Hebrew Piel is called Form II (Arabic speakers call it the *fa"ala*). As in Hebrew, it is formed by doubling the middle letter of the three-letter root and it has an intensive meaning: *qatala* is *he killed*, *qattala* is *he murdered*. Form III, which has no formal parallel in Hebrew, is *qaatala*, which means *he tried to kill*.

The remaining forms include various causative, reflexive and passive elaborations of the main verbal idea. Form IX is rare and unusual, being limited to verbal roots that express colours or defects, such as *ihmarra* (*it turned red*) and *iswadda* (*it turned black*).

Speakers of Indo-European languages have used grammaticalization processes to mark their verbs for tense and aspect, whereas the Semitic languages stand out partly because of aspect but chiefly on account of all these derived forms. One of the fascinating things about comparing languages is spotting these differences in expression, which might indicate that their speakers not only describe, but perhaps also view, the world in subtly different ways.

Turkic Languages

Turkey represents only the westernmost point reached by the speakers of a group of languages that actually originated far to the east.

While most people know that Turkish is spoken in Turkey, fewer people know that the Kazakh language of Kazakhstan is a Turkic language; so is the Azerbaijani of Azerbaijan, the Kyrgyz of Kyrgystan, the Chuvash of central Russia, the Uyghur of the Xinjiang Uyghur Autonomous Region of western China, the Dolgan of north Siberia and the Chulym of south Siberia – to name just a few. The original homeland of the Turkic speakers is a matter of debate, but was possibly somewhere in the north of modern Mongolia. At any rate, the earliest documents in any kind of Turkic language were found in Mongolia and date from the 8th century AD.

The map below shows the geographic distribution of the Turkic group. Although the languages are widespread, they are surprisingly similar to each other, which makes the establishment of genetic relationships between them problematic. It is simplest for our purposes

A manuscript written in the Ottoman Turkish alphabet, which was replaced by a Latin-based alphabet in 1928.

to stick to geographical designations. Some 160,000,000 people speak a Turkic language as their first language; about 40 percent of these speak Turkish. That leaves a large number speaking other varieties (see diagram opposite).

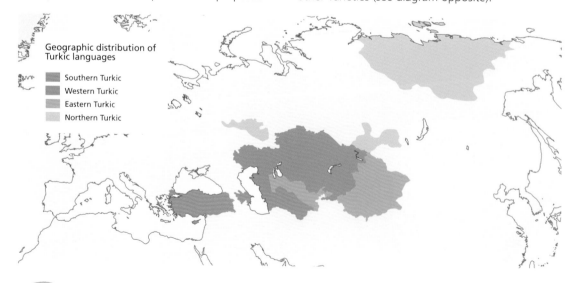

Geographic distribution of
Turkic languages

- Southern Turkic
- Western Turkic
- Eastern Turkic
- Northern Turkic

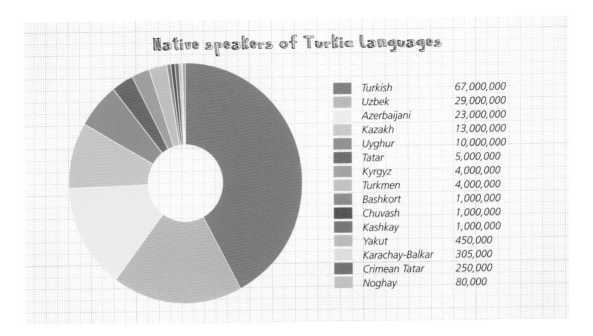

Native speakers of Turkic languages

Language	Speakers
Turkish	67,000,000
Uzbek	29,000,000
Azerbaijani	23,000,000
Kazakh	13,000,000
Uyghur	10,000,000
Tatar	5,000,000
Kyrgyz	4,000,000
Turkmen	4,000,000
Bashkort	1,000,000
Chuvash	1,000,000
Kashkay	1,000,000
Yakut	450,000
Karachay-Balkar	305,000
Crimean Tatar	250,000
Noghay	80,000

In common with other languages in the group, Turkish does not typically begin words with a cluster of more than one consonant. If Turks want to refer to the *scorpion fish*, they call it an *iskorpit*. In the same way, the word *ispirto* refers to alcohol, plainly borrowed from *spirit* in European languages.

Vowel harmony

Perhaps the most striking phonetic feature of all the Turkic languages is vowel harmony. This means that the quality of the first vowel in a word typically has an effect on that of all the subsequent vowels. Because this effect starts from the first syllable and works forward, it is an example of what linguists call *progressive assimilation*.

You have already seen that sounds can be classified by the place of their articulation (see Phonetics, page 24). If a vowel is made toward the front of the mouth, it is called a front vowel; if made toward the back, it is a back vowel. In either case, the height of the tongue also conditions the quality of the vowel.

If the tongue is close to the roof of the mouth, the vowel is close (or high); if the tongue is lowered, the vowel is open (or low). Intermediate positions are available in respect of backness, frontness, openness and closeness. Finally, the lips may be rounded or unrounded.

This means that the Turkish vowels can be classified as shown below (using for these purposes not the International Phonetic Alphabet but the modified Roman alphabet used in Turkey). The rounded vowels are lower case and the unrounded are upper case:

	Front		**Back**	
Close	i	Ü	ı	U
Open	e	Ö	a	O

The rules on harmony differ between the Turkic languages. For Turkish, the following apply (but with all sorts of tricky exceptions that you would have to follow up in a grammar book):

If the first vowel is ...	The following vowels will be ...
front	front
back	back
unrounded	unrounded
rounded	rounded and close; or unrounded and open

Turkic languages are not alone in having vowel harmony: it is also found in the Uralic languages, for example Finnish and Hungarian. Some linguists thought that these similarities were to be explained by grouping Turkic and Uralic languages into one giant Ural-Altaic macro-family. But that conclusion presupposed that Turkic was part of their so-called Altaic family, together with Mongolian. That widespread assumption was largely discredited in the 1960s by the Turcologist Sir Gerard Clauson, and it remains a minority view.

Words and word order

In terms of morphology, all the Turkic languages have in common the fact that they are agglutinating. That is to say that words are modified by adding sequences of sounds that generally cannot stand by themselves to form independent words (bound morphemes, in other words), but which mark things such as singular or plural, first or third person, possessive, and so on. For example, the word *akılsızlıklarından* means "because of their stupidity". It is made up systematically and logically starting from a basic noun *akıl* (*reason*, *rationality*) followed by a series of bound morphemes as follows: *-sız-* (*-less*), *-lık-* (*-ness*), *-larin-* (*their*), *-dan* (*because of*).

The usual word order is SOV (subject-object-verb, see page 58): so "Hasan told the story" would have to be ordered in Turkish as "Hasan the story told". Other permutations are possible, but they would only be used to give emphasis to a particular element in the sentence.

In the Turkic languages, is usual for a modifier to precede the thing modified (left-branching grammar): adjectives come before nouns and adverbs before verbs. There is also a tendency for adverbial expressions of time and place to come toward the beginning of the sentence, and for an indirect object to precede the direct object. So if you wanted to say "Sherlock Holmes unexpectedly revealed his suspicions to his brother ten days ago on board ship", the order of the elements in Turkish would be, "Sherlock Holmes ten days ago on board ship to his brother his suspicions unexpectedly revealed."

If we take the word *ev* (*house*), it has an unrounded front vowel. Turkish plurals are generally formed with the suffix *-ler* or *-lar*, depending on the preceding syllable. In this case, we must have *evler*; the form **evlar* would not be allowed since it involves a back vowel following a front one. The suffix *-de / -da* means *at* or *in*; so *evlerde* is correct for *in the houses*, but **evlerda* would violate vowel harmony.

Now contrast with this the word for *room*, *odad*. Both the vowels are back vowels. So *rooms* would have to be *odadlar*, not **odadler*, and *in the rooms* must be *odadlarda*, not **odadlarde*.

Language Families

This is not much more unusual than what we find in some other languages. The most confusing aspect of word order is perhaps where relative clauses are involved. If you want to say in Turkish "The student who goes to university on the bus", you have to say, "University-to bus-on go-ing student" That makes things difficult for speakers of many European languages, since the order of elements is almost the exact opposite of what you expect in French, Italian, Spanish or English.

Turkish (like English and Persian) has no grammatical gender, and neither do other Turkic languages. Unlike English, there is not even a separate Turkish pronoun for *he* or *she*; the word *o* does duty for both. For example, *onu seviyor* could mean *he loves her*, *she loves him*, *he loves him*, *she loves her*. In most contexts the ambiguity may be resolved by the use of an appropriate noun (mother, father, aunt, uncle and so on). But in poetry, for example, it might serve a purpose to retain deliberate ambiguity in some contexts.

Again in common with some other languages, Turkish regularly expresses possession without using a verb meaning *to have*. If you want to say *I don't have time* in Turkish, you say *zamanım yok*. In this sentence, *zaman* means *time*, *-ım* is a first person possessive suffix and *yok* is a word denoting non-existence. So a literal rendering is *time-my non-existent*.

Like English, Turkish has no grammatical gender. Unlike English, it does not have separate pronouns for *he* and *she*: the pronoun *o* is used for both, leaving plenty of room for ambiguity.

He loves him

She loves her

She loves him

He loves her

Uralic Languages

Estonian, Finnish and Hungarian do not have much in common with the languages spoken in their respective neighbouring countries. They are, however, related to each other.

If you go to Finland, you will find that Finnish (5 million speakers) does not look or sound like the Norwegian, Swedish and Russian spoken in the neighbouring countries. Hungarian (10 million speakers) is utterly unlike the German, Slovakian, Romanian, Serbian or Croatian of the surrounding states. You will not find many similarities between Estonian (1 million speakers) and its neighbours, Russian and Latvian. But Estonian, Finnish and Hungarian, although unrelated to the neighbours with whom they share land borders, turn out to be related to each other, as we can see from the following items of shared vocabulary:

	Estonian	Finnish	Hungarian
water	*vesi*	*vesi*	*víz*
fish	*kala*	*kala*	*hal*
eye	*silma*	*silmä*	*szem*
woman	*naine*	*nainen*	*nő*
two	*kaks*	*kaksi*	*kettő*
four	*neli*	*neljä*	*négy*

These three languages are the best known of a group linguists call Uralic. You might be surprised by just how widespread these languages are, even if they have relatively few speakers in global terms. For example, there are fewer than 40,000 speakers of Mordvin in Russia and perhaps only 2,000 speakers of all the Saami languages in Finland.

The odd one out

Looking at the examples given in the table above, you can see at once that Finnish and Estonian are closer to each other than either is to Hungarian. This is perhaps only to be expected, given the geographical proximity of the first two and the remoteness of Hungary from either. Just by looking at the map below, you can see that Hungarian is an outlier, conspicuously separated from the other Uralic languages that extend across a northern corridor from Scandinavia to Siberia. Given the many different influences that Hungarian must

Geographic distribution of Uralic languages

■ Baltic-Finnic
■ Saami
■ Ugric
■ Permic
■ Volgaic
■ Samoyedic

The Uralic case system

Ancient Greek looks tricky with its nominative, accusative, genitive and dative. Latin has an ablative as well. Sanskrit has nominative through ablative, plus instrumental and locative. Finnish, by contrast, has a staggering fifteen cases.

	SINGULAR ENDING	EXAMPLES
nominative	-0	*The car* is red
accusative	-0 / -n	I saw *the car*
genitive	-n	The colour *of the car* is yellow
essive	-na / -nä	They use that wheelbarrow *as a car*
translative	-ksi	She turned that wreck *into a car*
partitive	-(t)a / -tta	He is washing *the car* (incomplete)
inessive	-ssa / -ssä	He slept *in the car*
elative	-sta / -stä	He stole the radio *out of the car*
illative	-an / -en	She brought blankets *into the car*
adessive	-lla / -llä	I will meet you back *at the car*
ablative	-lta / -ltä	I walked *away from the car*
allative	-lle	We ran back *to the car*
abessive	-tta / -ttä	We manage very well *without a car*
comitative	-ne	He looks a fool *with that car*
instructive	-n	He rammed the garage door with *his car*

have undergone in its central European corridor, at the crossroads of so many languages and cultures, it is not surprising that it has undergone more marked sound changes.

That said, Hungarian shares with Finnish (and Estonian) a number of structural features that make their relationship pretty clear. The first is vowel harmony, which you have encountered in Turkish (see Turkic Languages, page 87). The second is agglutination, which is also characteristic of Turkish. The third is lack of grammatical gender, again found in Turkish. But this does not mean that the Uralic and Turkic languages are related – vocabulary differences alone put paid to that idea. The fourth and most striking feature that the Uralic languages all share, and Turkish does not, is a rich system of cases, as shown in the table above.

Finnish, for example, has 15 cases. Most other languages mark most of these features with prepositions, but the Uralic languages have taken grammaticalization to an entirely new level.

He is washing the truck   *He slept in the truck*

We ran back to the truck   *She brought blankets into the truck*

In Finnish, all the actions shown in the illustration above require the use of a different case.

Languages of the Caucasus

The Caucasus is a mountainous region bounded by the Black Sea to the west and the Caspian Sea to the east. It contains the entirety of Armenia, Azerbaijan and Georgia, and parts of southern Russia, eastern Turkey and northwestern Iran.

Lying between Europe and Asia, it is a place of extraordinary linguistic diversity. For this reason, it makes sense to take its languages together under one geographical heading rather than using the "family" approach adopted so far in this book.

Five major language families are found in the Caucasus. In the (non-exhaustive) list below, languages discussed elsewhere in the book are indicated by a page reference. The aim is just to illustrate the amazing variety of languages in the region, with an indication of numbers of speakers and places where spoken:

Turkic
Azerbaijani (9,000,000; Azerbaijan, see page 86)
Kumyk (400,000; Dagestan)

Indo European
Armenian (3,000,000; Armenia)
Ossetian (500,000; North Ossetia-Alania)
Russian (3,000,000; Georgia, see page 78)

Kartvelian
Georgian (3,000,000; Georgia)
Laz (20,000; Turkey)
Mingrelian (350,000; Georgia)
Svan (14,000; Georgia)

West Caucasian (or Abkhaz-Circassian)
Abaza (40,000; Russia)
Abkhaz (130,000; Georgia)

Adyghe (100,000; Russia)
Kabardian (500,000; Russia)

East Caucasian
Akhvakh (8,000; Russia)
Avar (700,000; Russia)
Bats (3,000; Georgia)
Bezhta (6,000; Russia)
Chechen (1,350,000; Russia)
Dargwa (490,000; Russia)
Dido (20,000; Russia)
Ingush (300,000; Russia)
Khinalugh (1,000; Azerbaijan)
Khvarshi (1,700; Russia)
Lak (180,000; Russia)
Lezgi (650,000; Russia)
Tabassaran (130,000; Russia)
Tsakhur (11,000; Russia)
Udi (4,000; Azerbaijan)

Language Families

Nowruz, the festival marking the beginning of spring on 31 March, is celebrated in the Caucasus countries and Azerbaijan, as well as in Iran and Afghanistan.

Consonants in Caucasian and Kartvelian languages

The West Caucasian languages are noted for having an enormous number of consonantal phonemes. After the end of the First World War, there were around 50,000 speakers of one of them, Ubykh, in Turkey, east of the Black Sea; the last known one died in 1992. Ubykh was said to have more than 80 consonantal phonemes but only two vowels. Abkhaz has more than 50 consonantal phonemes. Some examples of Abkhaz words are:

 z̧ʷ3ʹbæ̈ (ten)

ʹz̧ʷeˑz3 (eleven)

Ẓʷøʏʒ (twelve)

ăts̆ˇắɥœ̈rʒ (to speak)

aχʷωʃɛ (butter)

English, by contrast, has only 24 consonantal phonemes but 12 vowels and 8 diphthongs.

East and West Caucasian and Kartvelian languages all make some use of so-called glottalic ejective consonants. These are difficult for non-speakers of these languages to learn to make. They involve the initiation of a sound not by using the pulmonic airstream (which comes straight from the lungs) but by closing the glottis (see Human Evolution, page 16) and using it to force existing air out of the mouth. Rather surprisingly, these are

not all throaty clicks: you can have a glottalized [p'] or [t'], for example. This involves forming the consonant toward the front of the mouth and accompanying it with a glottal ejection in the pharynx. Try it at home, but be careful not to choke in the attempt!

Ergativity

An unusual morpho-syntactic feature of the East and West Caucasian and Kartvelian languages is that they make use of ergativity to differing degrees. This is a system where the direct object of a transitive verb (such as *dismiss*) stands in the same case – called the absolutive – as the subject of an intransitive verb (such as *resign*), whereas the subject of a transitive verb is put into the ergative case. So in an ergative language one might say:

A (*ergative case*) dismissed (*perfective verb*)
B (*absolutive case*);
but
B (*absolutive case*) resigned (*perfective verb*).

In Georgian, this kind of ergativity is found only when the verb is in the perfective aspect. In the imperfective, the system reverts to the more familiar nominative-accusative polarity:

A (*nominative case*) dismisses (*imperfective verb*)
B (*object case*);
and
B (*nominative case*) resigns (*perfective verb*)

This rather confusing state of affairs is called split ergativity.

Languages of India

The territorial vastness of India is matched by its majestic array of languages – some 420 indigenous living languages at the time of writing.

It is not uncommon to hear that there are basically just two macro-families present in India: a very large number of Indo-European languages in the north and a smaller number of Dravidian ones in the south. This is broadly correct, but misses the fact that many Tibeto-Burman languages are spoken in the northeast, in and around Assam and Manipur states, such as Boro (1.3 million speakers) and Meitei (1.5 million speakers). There are also about 6 million speakers of Austro-Asiatic languages such as Santhali in Bihar, Orissa, Assam and West Bengal.

The *official* languages of India for legislative and judicial purposes are Hindi and English, but there is no national language in the sense of one (or more)

Kashmiri
Punjabi
Nepali
Assamese
Nissi
Hindi
Khasi
Ao
Manipuri
Gujarati
Bhili
Marathi
Odia
Bengali
Mizo
Konkani
Telugu
Kannada
Malayalam
Tamil
Andaman Islands

This Indian miniature is a folio from the poet Bilvamangala's *Balagopalastuti*. It shows the poet himself chanting hymns to the blue figure of Krishna.

Language Families

that is recognized as somehow quintessentially Indian. With such variety, it is hard to see how there could be. There are 29 states in India and 7 so-called Union Territories. Each of these has the right to specify one or more official languages for itself; each has done so, with the result that 22 languages are recognized as having official status (there is some overlap). Of the 1.3 billion people living in India, approximately 75 percent speak a language of Indo-European type; 20 percent speak a Dravidian language; and the remaining 5 percent speak Tibeto-Burman, Austro-Asiatic and a small number of other varieties. The broad general picture can be gathered from the map opposite.

The earliest Indian languages

The earliest written remains of any Indian language are the Edicts of Aśoka, the third emperor of the Maurya dynasty. They date from the middle of the 3rd century BC and take the form of 33 texts inscribed mostly on pillars, but also on large stones and cave walls. They represent Aśoka's desire to spread around his empire the ethical precepts of the Buddhist faith, to which he had converted.

But this was by no means the earliest stage of the Indic languages. The so-called Vedic hymns are perhaps as much as a thousand years older. They were not committed to writing until the mid-14th century AD, having been transmitted purely orally before that time. The reason for this is that the hymns are sacred texts of the Hindu faith and their faithful oral transmission is a specific function of the Brahminic priestly class. You might wonder how we can know that the texts go back to the late 2nd millennium BC if they were not written down until the fourteenth century AD. The answer is that the

The Edicts of Aśoka

Some of the pillars inscribed with the Edicts of Aśoka in the 3rd century BC still survive in India today. The sandstone column below is at the site of the ancient city of Vaishali, in present-day Bihar.

techniques of historical linguistics show that the language is much older than that of the Aśokan inscriptions. Linguists know a great deal about the kinds of changes that languages undergo over time and quite a lot about how long such changes take. The language of the Vedic hymns can be shown to be in many respects more conservative – at least in consonantal phonology and some aspects of morphology and syntax – than the language of the Homeric epics, which many linguists would place in the 8th century BC. The language of the hymns is very similar to that of sacred texts composed in the early Iranian language Avestan. This is likewise not attested in manuscript form until AD 1288 (and some manuscripts are as much as 500 years older), but is generally thought to belong to the late 2nd millennium BC.

There is the additional fact that the Vedic hymns are composed in a variety of fairly strict poetic forms requiring a prescribed arrangement of heavy and light syllables. The fact that these are still correct after all this time tends to suggest that the transmission has for the most part been faithful. If the Brahmins had allowed everyday speech to creep in, the patterns would have been lost.

A 19th-century manuscript in Devanagari script of the Rigveda, a collection of Vedic Sanskrit hymns, some verses of which are still recited as prayers today.

Vedic has been a crucial element in the work of philologists trying to understand the Indo-European family of languages (see page 54). But it is also important as the fountainhead, in some sense, of all the later languages of India that belong in the Indo-European family. It would be simplistic to say that Hindi and Marathi and Punjabi and Gujarati and Konkani and Bhili and Sindhi and Kashmiri and Nepali and Sinhalese and Bengali and Assamese are all "daughter" languages of Vedic in the same way that the Romance languages are descended from Latin. But it is not so very far from the truth. We possess a continuous record not only of the evolution of Vedic into Classical Sanskrit, but also of the latter into the various Middle Indic varieties known collectively as Prakrits.

Development of the modern languages of India

One such Prakrit is Magadhi. It is used in the Classical Sanskrit dramas as a form of speech for low types of whom the audience is meant to disapprove. It is also the vehicle of the extensive literature of the Jain faith. Another Prakrit is Pali, which contains the voluminous corpus of texts of Theravada Buddhism. Examples of the changes between Sanskrit and Middle Indic are:

simplification of diphthongs: Sanskrit *śaurya* (*heroism*) vs. Pali *sōria*.
simplification of consonant clusters: Sanskrit *bhakta* (*food*) vs. Pali *bhatta*
loss of final consonants: Sanskrit *samyak* (*together*) vs. Pali *sammā* (with the *-my-* sequence also simplified to *-mm-*).

The modern languages of India have continued these changes. For example, the Sanskrit for *seven* was *sapta*; in Pali this was simplified to *satta*; in Hindi it has been simplified still further to *sāt*.

At the morphological level, Sanskrit has more inflected forms than any other Indo-European language: eight cases in the singular, dual and plural for nouns, and six tenses, three voices and five moods for verbs. The modern languages have tended toward simplification, making do with

Language Families

Billi (cat)
Urdu
بلی

Billi (cat)
Hindi
बिल्ली

fewer morphological categories. That said, the trend is not universal. Bengali is rather conservative, with four cases for nouns (nominative, accusative, genitive and locative).

The situation of Hindi and Urdu is interesting. It is not unusual to see them described as two languages, but on the spoken level they are virtually indistinguishable. A person who speaks Hindi can speak Urdu. The differences between them arise at the written level. Hindi is written in the Devanagari script that is common to many other Indian languages; Urdu (like Persian) is written in a modified form of the Arabic script. Not only are they written in different scripts, they draw on different kinds of vocabulary for their prose and poetry. Hindi draws on a more Sanskritic fund of words, but Urdu shows many influences from Arabic and Persian. For example, in spoken Hindi-

A Hindi speaker can understand a speaker of Urdu, but while their languages are almost indistinguishable on the spoken level, they look very different from each other when written.

Urdu the word for *book* is *kitāb*. This is a loan word from Arabic. Literary Urdu happily uses it, whereas literary Hindi prefers the Sanskritic *pustak*.

The Dravidian languages, such as Tamil, Kannada, Malayalam, Telugu and about 80 others, have very different phonological and morphological features from the Indo-European languages of India. The fact that they are found largely in the south, but with pockets in mountainous areas of the north, might suggest that speakers of Dravidian languages were present in India before speakers of Indo-European arrived, and were largely displaced southward by these incomers from the north.

Languages of India

Iranian Languages

Like the languages of India, the languages of Iran can be traced back to the second half of the 2nd millennium BC.

Archaeologists think that a recognizable Indo-Iranian group split away from the main Indo-European bloc in the steppes of eastern Europe some time around 3500 BC. Their move into Central Asia may be dated from about 2200 BC.
By this time, it seems that there was already a Proto-Iranian group in the north and a Proto-Indic one in the south. The Indic group pushed down into the Indian subcontinent from about 2000 BC. The Iranian group remained in Central Asia but moved westward into the region of modern Iran from about 1500 BC (see map opposite).

Old Iranian languages

The Old Iranian languages (Old Avestan, Younger Avestan and Old Persian) can be arranged in terms of time-depth and geographical spread, as shown in the diagram to the right. The Medes and Scythians are known to have existed because they are mentioned in historical sources from other countries in the region. The little that is known of

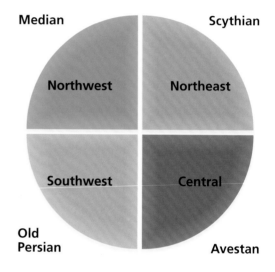

Median · Scythian
Northwest · Northeast
Southwest · Central
Old Persian · Avestan

their languages has to be deduced from the names of people and places.

Just as the earliest monuments of Indian languages are the Vedic hymns, so the earliest traces of Iranian are found in the so-called Gathas, a set of liturgical texts attributed to the prophet Zoroaster and composed in a variety of Iranian called Old Avestan. Although the Gathas are not

The Faravahar icon is a symbol of Zoroastrianism, the main religion of pre-Islamic Persia.

Language Families

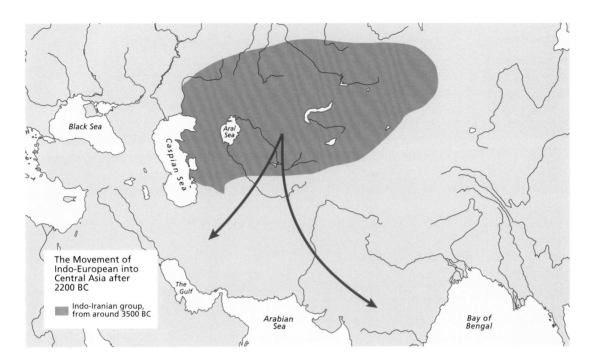

The Movement of Indo-European into Central Asia after 2200 BC

Indo-Iranian group, from around 3500 BC

attested in writing before AD 1000, they are plainly of the same order of antiquity as Vedic Sanskrit. They belong to the latter half of the 2nd millennium BC.

The following correspondences illustrate this:

Avestan	Vedic Sanskrit	English
pitar	pitar	father
dātar	dātar	giver
dva	dvā	two
frīnāmi	prīnāmi	I take delight in
yauuat	yāvat	as long
vastra	vastra-	clothing
tvə̄m	tvam	you (singular)

Many words are identical; others differ only according to predictable sound laws. The two languages are not the same, but they do offer plentiful evidence of a time when the Indic and Iranian languages were very close together.

An example of the oldest part of the Avesta (the Gathas), attributed to Zoroaster himself, is the lament of a cow before the gods about its poor treatment. It is very interesting for its content, but also for comparison with later Iranian languages.

Here are the first two verses:

Avestan	English
1a. xšmaibyā gə̄uš urvā gərəždā:	**1a.** To you (pl.) the cow's soul made lament:
1b. kahmāi mā θwarōždūm? kə mā tašaṭ	**1b.** For whom did you (pl.) fashion me? Who shaped me?
2a. ā mā ǣšəmō hazascā	**2a.** Madness and violence,
2b. rəmō āhišāyā dərə̄scā təvīšcā.	**2b.** Cruelty, ill-treatment and brutality have oppressed me.
3a. nōiṭ mōi vāstā xšmaṭ anyō	**3a.** There is no other herds-man for me but you (pl.):
3b. aθā mōi sąstā vohū vāstryā.	**3b.** therefore render me the good of pastures!

Looking at this early text from the latter part of the 2nd millennium BC, it is pretty staggering to find that some of the vocabulary items survived in a more or less recognizable form for a thousand years or more into Middle Persian texts written in Pahlavi, where the following correspondences can be seen:

Avestan	Pahlavi	English
gāuš < gav	gāw	cow
gərəždā	garzīd	complain
vohū	weh	good
vāstryā < vāstra	wāstar	pasture

Indeed, the word for *cow* in Modern Persian is *gāv* – which is from the same Indo-European root as English *cow*, German *Kuh*, Latin *bos*, Greek *bous* and English *bovine*.

Old Persian is attested a good deal later than Avestan but is still relatively ancient. It is attested from 522 BC, beginning with the inscriptions set up on Mount Behistun by the Persian king Darius I. When the king describes himself as *xšāyaθiya vazraka* (*great king*), you might distantly recognize in the adjective *vazraka* the forerunner of the New Persian *bozorg* (*big*), as spoken in modern Iran. There are other items in the language of these Old Persian inscriptions that likewise appear more than 1,500 years later in the earliest New Persian sources. For example, in his description of the building of the palace at Susa, Darius uses the words *kapauta* (*blue*), which is New Persian *kabūdī*; *sinkabruš* (*vermilion*), which is New Persian *šangarf*; *abary* (*brought*), which is the same root as New Persian *bar-* (*carry*) and *hačā* (*from*), which eventually gives New Persian *az* (and, more recognizably, Balochi *ač*). Much pioneering work in identifying these historical changes through the often confusing pathways of Middle Iranian was done by the great scholar of Indian and Iranian, Professor Sir Harold Bailey (1899–1996).

Developments in Middle Iranian

So just as the Middle Indo-Aryan Prakrits started to diverge from various varieties of Old Indic, so the Old Iranian languages, spread over time and space, underwent their own independent evolutions as they turned into a broad variety of Middle Iranian languages (see diagram below).

It is important to appreciate that the Old and Middle Iranian-speaking zone is divided into two definite dialectal areas: the western zone, which includes modern Iran, and the eastern zone, which covers much of Central Asia. Whereas Indic languages are, and always have been, spoken in the area that corresponds roughly with the modern

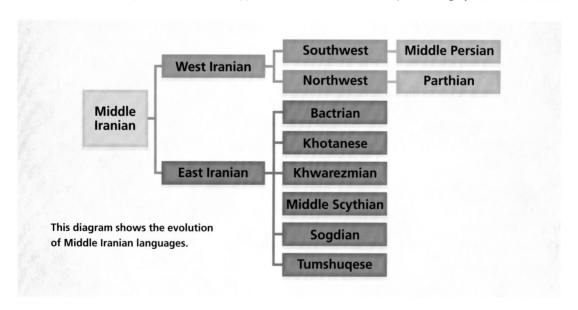

This diagram shows the evolution of Middle Iranian languages.

Language Families

In this portrait, the great Indo-Iranian philologist Professor Sir Harold Bailey (1899–1996) is shown wearing a traditional woollen coat from the Caucasus.

Few living people know the Middle Iranian language called Sogdian. It is the vehicle of important texts concerning Christianity and Manichaeanism (the faith of the Iranian prophet Mani from the 3rd century AD). Sogdian texts date chiefly from the 9th and 10th centuries AD. A variety of Sogdian is still spoken today in Tajikistan, in the language called Yaghnobi.

The situation changed radically for the Iranian languages with the Islamic conquest of much of Central Asia. We can see this in the adoption of the Arabic alphabet, which is not especially suited for writing Persian because Arabic has a number of phonemes that do not appear in Persian, and so a number of varieties of /s/, /z/, /h/ and /t/ are written with no correspondence to the phonetic realities of spoken Persian.

Modern Persian

For the most part, Modern Persian (like English) has a very simplified system of inflection. Apart from the verb, which is inflected in an extremely predictable way, there is little morphological complexity: no grammatical gender, no agreement of adjectives, a very limited set of plural markers, no case marking except for a particle -rā that follows the direct object of a verb. Into this picture came the much greater inflectional complexity of Classical Arabic: nouns have all kinds of irregular (or "broken") plurals, and verbs have a bewildering array of inflectional markers going far beyond mere tense and person.

People often compare this to the way that English, which is basically a Germanic language, acquired lots of words from Latin and French. But the difference is that those external influences were all Indo-European. Persian is basically an Indo-European language, whereas Arabic is Semitic, so the latter's influence on the former is of an entirely different kind.

nation-state of India, the Iranian languages have never been coterminous with the (admittedly very large) area covered by modern Iran. In fact, forms of Iranian speech have been present from as far west as Turkey to as far east as China. The extraordinary cultural efflorescence that took place in Central Asia in the 11th century AD, making Bukhara, Samarqand, Balkh and Merv into mighty cultural centres to rival Baghdad during the Abbasid Caliphate, was to a large extent driven by people who spoke and wrote in Persian.

Languages of Africa

**Serious work on the more than 2,000 languages
of this vast continent did not get under way
until the late 19th century.**

It was the pioneering American linguist Joseph Greenberg (see Other Language Families, page 63) who suggested in the 1950s that the languages of Africa could be grouped into four large macro-families as follows:
1. Afro-Asiatic
2. Niger-Kordofanian, nowadays called Niger-Congo
3. Nilo-Saharan
4. Khoisan (a problematic label, as we shall see on page 105)

You can see on the map below the approximate regions where languages in these four major groups are spoken.

In total, more than 2,000 languages are spoken in Africa. To suggest that such a diverse group of languages can be reduced in the end to only four groups, as Greenberg suggested, is bold, to put it mildly. We now need to consider some of the problems in classification that are caused by the sheer variety of the material.

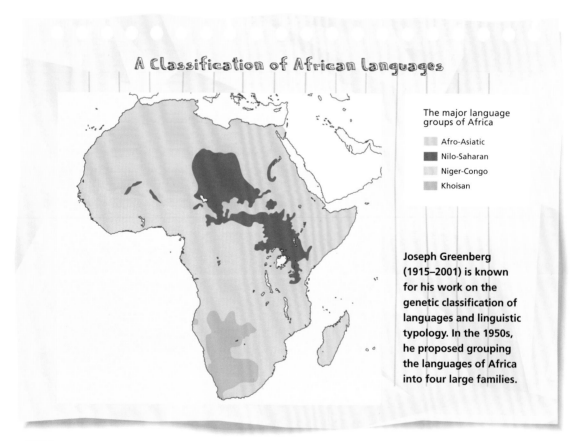

A Classification of African languages

The major language groups of Africa

- Afro-Asiatic
- Nilo-Saharan
- Niger-Congo
- Khoisan

Joseph Greenberg (1915–2001) is known for his work on the genetic classification of languages and linguistic typology. In the 1950s, he proposed grouping the languages of Africa into four large families.

Afro-Asiatic languages

The Afro-Asiatic group contains the subset of Semitic languages (see page 82). Of these, Arabic is spoken across much of North Africa, from Egypt in the east to Morocco in the west. The varieties spoken on the streets (as opposed to the Arabic used in news broadcasts and other formal settings) are very different, to the point where the ordinary speech of Cairo is not intelligible in Rabat. The number of people in Africa who speak some variety of Arabic as their mother tongue is in the order of 120,000,000. This contrasts with only about 80,000,000 in the Middle East. Also belonging to the Semitic family are Amharic, Tigrinya, Tigre and Gurage; they are part of the Ethiopic branch. Amharic has some 40,000,000 speakers in Ethiopia and Tigrinya around 8,000,000 in Eritrea.

Beside these Semitic languages, but just as much a part of the Afro-Asiatic group, are Egyptian and the Berber, Chadic, Cushitic and Omotic subgroups. Speakers of Berber languages are spread across much of North Africa, including Algeria, Libya, Mali, Morocco and Niger. Reliable statistics are hard to come by because censuses conducted in these countries do not always record numbers of Berber speakers. An overall and very rough median estimate for the whole of Africa would be in the range of 20,000,000 people.

Unlike earlier forms of Egyptian, Coptic was written in a version of the Greek alphabet, with the addition of some letters based on demotic signs.

Egyptian is no longer spoken, of course, being the language of the ancient Egyptians which died out in the first few centuries AD. That said, it had a continuous recorded history in writing for some 3,500 years and is important for the light it throws on the group as a whole. It also lives on in Coptic, which, although no longer an everyday spoken language, remains in use for religious purposes among the Coptic Christians of Egypt.

In ancient Egypt, hieroglyphic writing was used for inscriptions on monuments and temples.

I think there's a spelling mistake...

The Cushitic languages number about 50 and have some 60,000,000 speakers in the Horn of Africa (Ethiopia, Eritrea, Somalia, Djibouti, Sudan). Oromo has about 45,000,000 speakers, most of whom live in Ethiopia, with the majority of the rest in Kenya. Somali has about 20,000,000 native speakers in Somalia.

The Chadic subgroup comprises about 150 languages spoken in Chad, Niger, Nigeria, Cameroon and the Central African Republic. The best known of these is Hausa, with around 22,000,000 speakers as a first language and many more who use it as a *lingua franca*.

Some of the shared features that linguists see as diagnostic of membership of the Afro-Asiatic language family include a marked similarity in pronouns, the sharing of a number of case endings on nouns, and a tendency to double consonants within the root of verbs. The status of the so-called Omotic subgroup in Ethiopia has been a subject of debate for some time because it is not clear how far, if at all, many members of this group exhibit these typical features.

Niger-Congo languages

Niger-Congo languages are undoubtedly predominant in terms of numbers. In total there are more than 1,400 such languages spoken by around 360,000,000 people across the vast area from Senegal in the west to Kenya in the east, and from Nigeria in the north to South Africa in the south. This makes it by far the largest language family on Earth. As you can see from the map, Niger-Congo languages are spoken across practically all of sub-Saharan Africa. Yoruba and Igbo are major languages in Nigeria. The Bantu subgroup is the largest single division and covers an enormous territory; some of the best-known Bantu languages are Shona, Swahili, Xhosa and Zulu.

Members of the Niger-Congo family have a number of shared features. Many exhibit vowel harmony (see Turkic Languages, page 87), although this is by no means unique to this group. Labiovelar sounds (such as [gw] and [kw]) are conspicuously rare in Bantu languages. There are similarities in the ways that nouns are marked with prefixes according to whether they are classified as human, animal, single, liquid, massive or having various other characteristics. The task of spotting family likenesses is not easy given the enormous number of languages involved and the length of time they have had to evolve; but most linguists are content that it makes sense to think of this group as a real and coherent entity.

Nilo-Saharan languages

Nilo-Saharan, by contrast, is a somewhat controversial group, found as it is only in isolated pockets in Sudan, Chad, Niger and Libya, among other places. Statistics are, for reasons already discussed, unsatisfactory and very approximate: perhaps some 30,000,000 people speak a Nilo-Saharan language as their mother tongue. The approximate distribution can be seen from the map. Whereas many African languages are assigned to families on the basis of shared features, such as word order, verbal morphology or noun categories, the Nilo-Saharan group depends only on a number of shared vocabulary items and morphemes. It is true that these seem to go beyond mere accident, but it is not encouraging that more fundamental structural similarities have been harder to find.

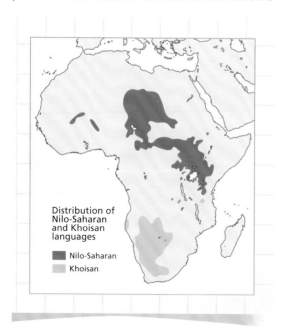

Distribution of Nilo-Saharan and Khoisan languages

■ Nilo-Saharan
■ Khoisan

Language Families

Click sound

1. **To make a click, the speaker breathes in and forms a closure at the front of the mouth using the front of the tongue, or, sometimes, lips.**

2. **A second closure is simultaneously made at the back of the mouth using the back part of the tongue.**

3. **A vacuum is then produced by drawing the tongue downward and backward.**

4. **When the front closure is released, swiftly followed by the back, air rushes in and the click results.**

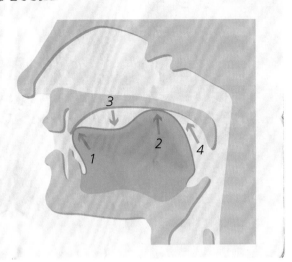

Khoisan languages

The Khoisan languages are spoken across much of the southwest, from Angola through Botswana and Namibia and down into northern South Africa. They are, if anything, even more controversial a category than Nilo-Saharan. Once labelled the "Bushman-Hottentot" languages, they number only 30 or so and have only a few hundred thousand speakers.

The term "Khoisan" is an umbrella: the languages do not form one coherent family but embrace perhaps four smaller groupings and a couple of isolated languages unrelated to any others. They all have in common a complex phonetic system involving clicks, which are made while breathing in. Although all the Khoisan languages include clicks, not all click languages are Khoisan. The Bantu languages Xhosa and Zulu have them, as does the Cushitic Dahalo. So clicks might be an areal rather than a genetic feature (see Other Language Families, page 62).

The precise sound depends on the nature of the front closure (whether lips, teeth, alveolar ridge and so on). The situation is more complex because clicks may be accompanied by a velar, pharyngeal or other articulation. The operation of these features together produces an enormous variety of clicked articulations.

Languages of the Pacific

The most striking linguistic feature about this region is the sheer variety that it presents. Many hundreds of languages are spoken on the islands of Oceania.

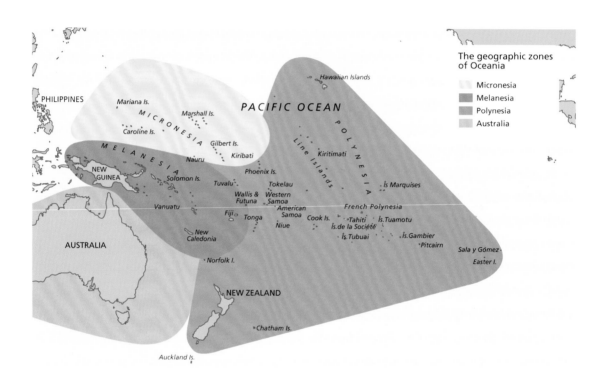

The geographic zones of Oceania

- Micronesia
- Melanesia
- Polynesia
- Australia

In referring to the languages of the Pacific, I do not mean the countries of the Pacific Rim, such as the west coasts of Canada, North America and South America, or the east coast of China or Japan. I am thinking instead of the many islands, large and small, that form part of Oceania. They have traditionally been classified geographically into four zones (see map above): Australia; Melanesia (for example, Fiji, Papua New Guinea and the Solomon Islands); Micronesia (for example, Kiribati and the Marshall Islands); and Polynesia (for example, Hawaii, New Zealand and Tonga).

Linguists generally divide the languages of the Pacific into three large groups:

1. Australian
2. Austronesian
3. Papuan

Australian languages

Of the 200 or so living indigenous languages (other than English) spoken in Australia, perhaps two-thirds will be extinct within a generation or two.

It is tricky to generalize about Australian languages. Quite a lot of them have a dual marker for nouns describing things that come in pairs naturally or by chance. There is generally also a system of suffixes used to indicate the case of nouns, for example, subject, direct object, indirect

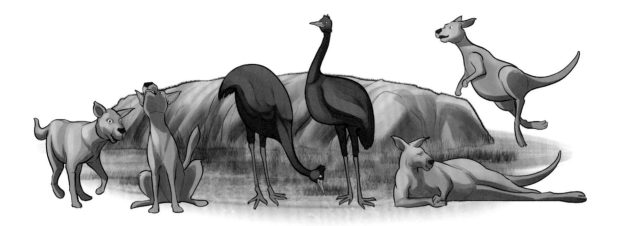

Many of the indigenous languages of Australia have a specific marker for nouns describing things – or animals – that come in pairs.

object, possessive. A good number of Australian languages have markers on the noun for ergativity, which you have already come across in the languages of the Caucasus (see page 93).

A typologically unusual feature exhibited by many languages in this region is considerable freedom of word order. This is not simply a correlate of having a clear system of case-markers on nouns. You have already seen in the case of Latin, for example, that there are six ways of arranging a sentence consisting of subject, object and verb (see Other Language Families, page 58 and Germanic Languages, page 74); but the fact remains that the statistically predominant word order in Latin is SOV. More or less complete freedom in word order is quite uncommon and hard to explain.

When most people think of Australia, it is not long before they think of the kangaroo. There is a myth that the word never did refer to the famous marsupial, but was a misunderstanding by Captain Cook's men when they met speakers of the Guugu Yimidhirr language in the far north of Queensland in the 1770s. The story goes that someone pointed to a kangaroo and asked what it was and received the answer *gaŋurru* (ŋ = ng), allegedly meaning "I don't understand" (or, less plausibly, "I don't

know"). This story, although amusing, is sadly untrue. It is correct that some later visitors to Australia could not get anyone to confirm that this name went with the springy animal, but that is not surprising, given that even within just one of the many Australian languages, there can be numerous words for different species of kangaroo. In the 1970s, the American anthropologist John Haviland confirmed that *gaŋurru* did indeed refer to the large, bouncy marsupial.

Behind this apparently trivial story is a much more interesting point about phonetics. Apart

The Captain and the Kangaroo

Contrary to popular belief, the word "kangaroo" is not based on a communication problem: when Captain Cook and his men asked the Guugu Yimidhirr people what they called this large marsupial, their reply did not mean "I don't understand".

In the Dharug language, Australia's second-most-famous marsupial is known as the *gula.*

from the kangaroo (and Foster's lager), perhaps the most famous emblem of Australia is the koala. Its name is also written in English with a /k/. But just as *kangaroo* is actually *gaɲurru* in Guugu Yimidhirr, *koala* is really *gula* in the Dharug language of New South Wales. It is not that Guugu Yimidhirr or Dharug have no voiceless stops [*k, p, t*] but only voiced stops [*g, b, d*]; it is rather that the distinction between the sets is not important. It is phonetic, but not phonemic (see Phonology, page 29) and is determined by the environment in which the stop occurs.

This lack of phonemic distinction between voiced and voiceless stops is typical of very many Australian languages. Another remarkable feature of most languages in this group is that they are almost entirely without fricatives (*f, v, s, z,* and so on). This absence is otherwise found only rarely – in Papua New Guinea and parts of South America. This fact is another demonstration that languages might share typological features without necessarily being related.

Austronesian languages

The Austronesian family is, after the Niger-Congo group in Africa, the second largest on Earth in terms of numbers of languages. It contains perhaps 1,000 languages, of which 450 or so are spoken within the Pacific basin. The remainder are found in Madagascar, Malaysia and Taiwan and parts of continental Asia.

The Babatana language of the Solomon Islands has 7,000 speakers. In common with many languages in this region, it has no affixes to mark verbs for tense (past, present, future) or aspect (see Slavonic Languages, page 80). This does not mean that these languages do not have ideas of time; they are simply expressed by using an independent word, typically a proclitic (a word with no accent of its own that sits before another word). This means that, with respect to verbs at least, some Austronesian languages are isolating (see Morphology, page 40). This feature is not unique to this group, but is found also in Chinese, for example.

The Yélî Dnye language spoken on remote Rossel Island in the Solomon Sea is notable for a unique consonant sound found in no other known language.

Language Families

The world's most linguistically diverse country

More than 830 languages are spoken on the islands, archipelagos and atolls that make up Papua New Guinea. Some languages are spoken by hundreds of thousands of people, others only by a few hundred. This diversity is probably due to the geographic and cultural isolation of different speech communities.

Papuan languages

The Papuan group does not represent a genetic family. It is simply a way of referring to the astonishing number of languages spoken on Papua New Guinea and the surrounding islands. Some of these are, in fact, Austronesian; others are related to other Papuan languages, and yet others are isolates. More than 830 languages are spoken in an area of 463,000 square kilometres (179,000 square miles) by about 8 million people (that is about the same population as New York City). This makes Papua New Guinea the most linguistically diverse place on the planet. Perhaps a hundred or more of these languages are spoken by groups of only a few hundred people. Around a dozen of them are spoken by groups that number from the low tens of thousands into the low hundreds of thousands. It is hard to explain this variety, but it probably has to do with isolation (both geographical and cultural) between small village speech communities, so that the centrifugal forces of change that affect all languages work more thoroughly, unchecked by centralizing forces.

The Yélî Dnye language is spoken by about 3,500 people on Rossel Island, part of an archipelago east of Papua New Guinea. It is unique among all known languages in possessing a particular kind of doubly articulated consonant. Double articulation means that a sound has two simultaneous places of articulation: all the click sounds in the Khoisan languages (see page 105) are doubly articulated because the tongue makes a frontal and rear closure at the same time. What is unique in Yélî Dnye is that it has labial-alveolar stops that contrast phonemically with labial-post-alveolar ones. An example is t͡pənə (*lung*) vs. t͡pənə (*horn*). In each case, there is not a [t] followed by a [p], but the simultaneous articulation of [t͡p] together. This is hard enough in itself, but it must be very difficult for foreigners to make or even perceive the difference between two such clusters when the only difference is that, in the latter, the tongue is slightly farther back in the mouth when making the [t] part of the sound. And yet to native speakers this distinction is plain enough to be used to separate words that in all other respects are the same.

Languages of Mainland Southeast Asia

Although they have different roots, there are striking similarities between many of the languages spoken in this region.

Mainland Southeast Asia consists of Myanmar, Cambodia, Laos, Thailand, Vietnam and peninsular Malaysia. This large area has five indigenous language families: Austronesian, Hmong-Mien, Mon-Khmer, Sino-Tibetan and Tai-Kadai. These are not coterminous with modern national borders; there is considerable overlap, as you can see from the map on the right.

What is striking about this part of the world is that many of its languages share structural similarities even though they are genetically unrelated. You have already encountered the phenomenon of areal influence (see Other Language Families, page 62), and it is particularly prominent in this part of the world. Its significance

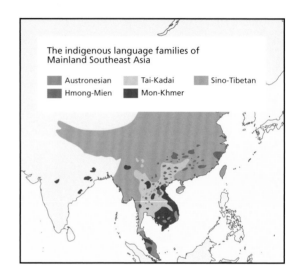

The indigenous language families of Mainland Southeast Asia

- Austronesian
- Hmong-Mien
- Tai-Kadai
- Mon-Khmer
- Sino-Tibetan

Tonal variations

ghost

rice seed

horse

tomb

ma

ma

Unlike other languages in the Mon-Khmer group, Vietnamese is tonal. Depending on how the word *ma* is said – whether the voice goes up, down or stays the same, for example – it can mean a number of very different things.

Language Families

is that it offers a very different perspective on the relations between languages from the model that was designed (and works well) to describe the Indo-European languages. In the latter family, many of the subgroups (Indic, Hellenic, Italic, Germanic) parted company several thousand years ago and, although not immune to areal influences, have largely kept recognizable structures that differentiate them from neighbouring but unrelated forms of speech (for example, Greek as compared with Arabic or Turkish). In the case of Mainland Southeast Asia, by contrast, speakers of genetically very different languages have been in contact in a relatively confined space for some millennia, and horizontal borrowings have taken place. Their causes and extent are highly controversial.

Tonality

Perhaps the most debated topic is tonality. This means that any given syllable – let us say (in a made-up example) *tan* – could have its syllabic nucleus (see Phonology, page 31) pronounced with the voice going up (*tán*); or going down (*tàn*); or going up and then down (*tân*); or staying at the same pitch throughout (*tān*), to mean different things in each case. This is just one kind of system, but fewer or more tones are possible. In theory, any syllable could have *x* different tones and thus *x* different meanings. The various forms of *tan* given here are called tonemes, and this kind of tonality is known as contour tonality. It differs from register tonality, in which the different tonemes are each pronounced at a different pitch rather than the voice going up and down or up and down within the same syllabic nucleus (see Chinese, page 113 and Japanese, page 117). You may well find elements of both contour and register tonality in the same language.

Vietnamese was long a topic of puzzlement to linguists. It belongs genetically in terms of vocabulary and structure to the Mon-Khmer group. Tonality is generally absent in Mon-Khmer. But Vietnamese has it – six different kinds, in fact, in the northern variety.

The precise mechanism by which the tones were acquired in Vietnamese is hotly debated. Most linguists consider that the "idea" of tonality is acquired from speakers of neighbouring languages that are tonal. Tai-Kadai and Hmong-Mien languages have complex tonal systems. Once the idea is applied, tonality manifests itself in forms that are determined by the phonology of the adoptive language. It would appear, for example, that there is a relationship between the voicing, or lack of it, of initial and final stops (for example, *pop*, *pob*, *bop*, *bob*) and the contour of the tone that sits on the intervening vowel.

Vowels, monosyllables and cases

Other possibly areal features of languages in this region might be the possession of a large inventory of different vowels, phonemic distinctions between long and short vowels, and a marked preference for monosyllabic words.

As you would expect, languages with monosyllabic words are isolating (see Morphology, page 40). They lack inflection. There is a widespread absence of marking nouns for gender, number and case, and verbs for tense and aspect. Of course, not all the languages in the area have all these characteristics. It is precisely because some do not that we can identify areal influences against features that are inherited from proto-languages.

The languages of this region show a preference for monosyllabic words, as evidenced by this menu listing various roast meats for sale on a Vietnamese food cart.

Chinese

China is a country of some 1.4 billion people, and Chinese is an umbrella term for their numerous varieties of speech.

Varieties of spoken Chinese

- Northern dialects (Mandarin)
- Wu dialects
- Xiang dialects
- Gan dialects
- Jin dialects
- Kejia dialects
- Yue dialects (Cantonese)
- Northern & Southern Min

The first-known examples of Chinese script are found on oracle bones from the Shang dynasty, which list information about rulers, events and religious rites.

Most people have heard of Cantonese (or Yuè), spoken in the south of China and Hong Kong. Many people are also aware that the official national language is Mandarin, spoken in the north by about 70 percent of all Chinese and originally the dialect of Beijing. But there are also other varieties thaat are spoken across large regions, such as Jin, Gàn, Xiāng, Hakka, Wù and Mĭn.

None of these varieties is mutually intelligible to a speaker of any of the others. Mandarin and Cantonese differ from each other at least as much as English and Dutch. It is only the unique Chinese writing system that provides unity across the enormous geo-political entity that is China. It does this because the characters have no necessary connection with the sounds of the words they

denote. Just as an English person sees 4 and says *four*, whereas an Italian says *quattro*, so a speaker in Beijing sees 我 (meaning *I*) and says *wǒ*, whereas a person in Kowloon says *ngo*.

Early forms of Chinese

The history of Chinese is difficult to investigate. The earliest written materials are characters carved into the so-called oracle bones (see image above), which date from 1300 BC to 1050 BC. These give practically no information about the history of the spoken language because the graphic symbols used are generally not phonetic in nature. The only clues to pronunciation are sparse. In part, for Old Chinese, there is the poetry of the *Shijing*, a collection of some 300 poems dating from the first half of the 1st millennium BC. Tradition says that these poems rhymed. Rhyme was important to Chinese poets and, for the much later period of Middle Chinese, we find entire rhyming dictionaries. The earliest of these is called *Qièyun* and dates from AD 601. It mentions half a dozen other such works, but none has survived. The method used by the compilers was to take a character and to explain it in terms of other characters. This only works, of course, if you know the pronunciation of these other characters. We do not. All we have is a series of equations telling us that character A sounds like the onset of the word denoted by character B and the nucleus and coda (see page 31) of the word denoted by character C, which is useless unless you already know what B and C sound like.

A significant breakthrough was made by the Swedish philologist Bernhard Karlgren. He applied the techniques of historical linguistics that had been developed for Indo-European languages to reconstruct what Chinese might have sounded like in the 7th century AD. He did this by taking a given character and looking at its contemporary pronunciation in the chief languages of north, south, east and west China. If they all agreed on the same initial sound, he assumed that this sound had been the same at the time of the *Qièyun*. If they differed, he used his knowledge of language change in other languages to guess the likely direction of travel. For example, if three Chinese languages agreed that the onset of a given syllable was [t], but three different ones had [d], Karlgren assumed that [d] was original. It is much more common for a voiced sound to lose its voicing than for a voiceless one to acquire it.

In this way, although he was not able to unravel all the problems, he made enormous headway in recovering some of the sounds of Old Chinese. Later work has shown that many of Karlgren's assumptions are doubtful or mistaken. The speech variety that he was reconstructing was not really that of any one place and time. Allowance must

Bernhard Karlgren

Bernhard Karlgren (1889–1978) was one of the greatest scholars of his time. As an undergraduate at Uppsala University, he studied Swedish dialects, but soon decided to extend the same methods of comparative phonetic reconstruction to Chinese instead. In 1910, having studied the language for two months, he went to China for the first time, where he studied Chinese dialects for two years. Karlgren's work on archaic Chinese shaped the field of Sinology for decades.

also be made for the compilers having used some archaic forms or some forms from territories slightly outside their own. Edwin Pulleyblank also showed that Karlgren had not taken enough account of other languages in the Sino-Tibetan group.

How self-contained is Chinese?

Chinese is generally presented as a cultural and historical monolith. It is often said to have affected the surrounding languages without having undergone any influence from the speech of non-Han peoples in surrounding areas. Although Chinese isolationism is not a myth, it is hard to believe that Chinese was at all times hermetically isolated from the speech of peoples in what are now Mongolia, Myanmar, Laos, Vietnam and Tibet. The current and vast territorial expanse of China did not reach the maximum we know today until almost 1800, by which time the Qing government had been fighting a series of very successful wars of expansion for almost half a century.

Examples of loan words into Chinese have been identified by various linguists. It is generally agreed that the Chinese word for *lion*, *shīzǐ*, is probably a borrowing from Tocharian *śiśäk*. The word sits oddly in Classical Chinese, where monosyllables

This 8th-century painting shows bandits holding up travellers on the Silk Road. It is from Dunhuang, the most westerly Chinese trading town on the route.

are the norm; the geographical situation of Tocharian speakers in Chinese Turkestan makes the borrowing likely; and the travels of Tocharians along the Silk Road makes it all the more probable.

Monosyllables and isolation

However that may be, the language as you currently find it has structures very different from those of the languages of Europe and the Middle East. The most striking thing about Chinese is its basically monosyllabic nature. In Classical Chinese, there tends to be a 1:1 relationship between word and morpheme. In modern Mandarin, very many of the words have two syllables – but this does not really mark a change in the quality of Chinese because these words are generally compounds. Thus *diànhuà* means *telephone* but is actually a

Language Families

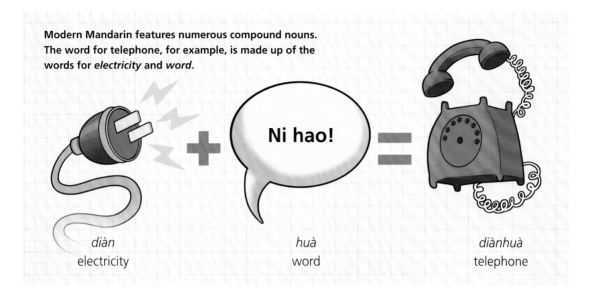

Modern Mandarin features numerous compound nouns. The word for telephone, for example, is made up of the words for *electricity* and *word*.

Ni hao!

diàn
electricity

huà
word

diànhuà
telephone

compound of two words, *diàn* meaning *electricity* and *huà* meaning *word*. There are only a very few disyllabic words in Chinese that cannot be analysed into monosyllabic compound elements: examples are *méiguì* (*rose*) and *zhīzhū* (*spider*).

As a result, the language is what linguists call isolating or analytic. This means that there is nothing in the way of inflection: no case endings on nouns and no inflection of verbs to indicate tense, aspect or mood. It is not that these ideas are absent from the language, but they are marked by adding particles before or after words in order to make the meaning clear. A typical sentence might look like this:

tā	**hē**	**le**	**shuǐ**	**ma**
3rd person singular	*drink*	*PAST*	*water*	*QUESTION*

"Has he drunk water?"

There is no word for *he* as opposed to *she*; *tā* indicates the third person; *shuǐ* is understood as the object because of word order and sense; *le* is a particle indicating a completed action; *ma* indicates a question. The meaning of the sentence depends on a series of meaningful words (drink, water), particles conveying syntactic information (completion, questioning) and word order.

Like the Tai-Kadai languages of Southeast Asia, Chinese is tonal. It has four tones: level (ā), rising (á), falling and rising (ǎ) and falling (à). These contour tones may be applied to a single syllable and result in four quite different meanings. Applying them to *yao*, for example, yields the following results: *yāo* (*to invite*), *yáo* (*to shake*), *yǎo* (*to bite*) or *yào* (*medicine*). You also find homophones within one and the same tone: thus *yāo* can also mean *evil spirit* or *waist* and *yáo* can also mean *ballad* or *kiln*.

Japanese

In spite of similarities between their writing systems, Japanese is not at all like Chinese.

Chinese is tonal; Japanese is not. Chinese is predominantly made up of words of one or two syllables; Japanese is not. Chinese has a tendency toward closed syllables, Japanese toward open. Chinese is an isolating language; Japanese is agglutinative (see Morphology, page 40) with elaborate systems of inflection.

Connections with other languages

The genetic affiliations of Japanese are a matter of dispute. Its speakers are concentrated in Japan and, although there are many in Australia, Brazil and Hawaii, that results from recent migrations and has nothing to tell us about the origins of the language. Many linguists treat it effectively as an isolate – a language with no relatives elsewhere. But *Homo sapiens* did not first come into being in Japan, so early humans must have arrived there from somewhere else. There was still a land bridge between Japan and Asia during the Upper Palaeolithic period (50,000–10,000 years ago), as shown on the map below. Some linguists see connections between Japanese and Korean at a level that goes beyond mere loan words or the borrowing of structures under areal influence. A minority even subscribe to the Altaic hypothesis, which would have Japanese and Korean as part of a group including Mongolian and Turkish (see Other Language Families, page 64). But even the relatively modest attempt to relate Japanese to Korean is problematic because the shapes of the two languages are so different. Japanese has predominantly open syllables (see Phonology, page 31), especially in the older phases of the language, which must be relevant to any historical inquiry;

Japan in Japanese is *Nihon*. The first of the two Japanese characters (or *kanji*) above means *sun* (*ni*), the second means *origin* (*hon*), hence "The Land of the Rising Sun".

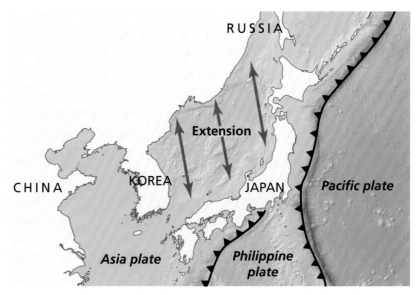

RUSSIA

Extension

CHINA

KOREA

JAPAN

Pacific plate

Asia plate

Philippine plate

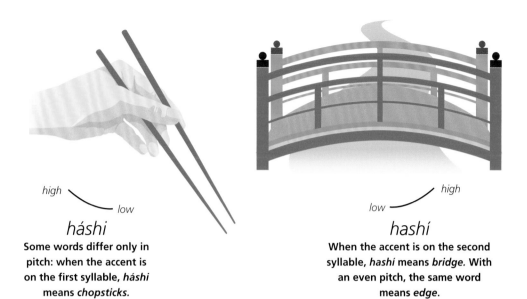

high ⟍
___ *low*

háshi

Some words differ only in pitch: when the accent is on the first syllable, *háshi* means *chopsticks*.

low ⟋ *high*

hashí

When the accent is on the second syllable, *hashí* means *bridge.* With an even pitch, the same word means *edge*.

Korean is quite the opposite, with mostly closed syllables. It is not easy to see how they could both have arisen from a common ancestor.

Pitch

Whereas Chinese is a language with contour tones, Japanese has pitch. The difference is simple but requires explanation. A Chinese tone can operate within a single syllable. Thus Chinese *má* is distinguished from *mǎ* in that in the former the voice goes up, whereas in the latter it goes down and up again. Both of these movements happen within the confines of a single syllable. Japanese pitch is quite different – here, a given syllable is pronounced at a higher musical pitch than another syllable following it. So pitch is about the prominence given to a particular syllable by elevation in musical terms; it has nothing to do with movement up and down within a single syllable. But the effect can be startling, because words that sound the same when pronounced in isolation can have quite different senses when followed by another syllable. Take the Japanese word *hi*: by itself it might have many meanings (for example, *sun, fire, princess, tombstone*). The sentence *hi ga deta* means "the sun has come out", whereas *hí ga deta* means "fire has broken out".

Hi ga deta
The sun has come out

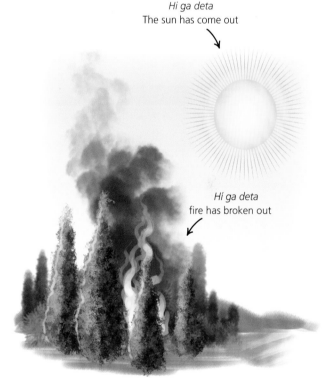

Hí ga deta
fire has broken out

Spoken in isolation, the Japanese word *hi* can mean sun or fire, among other things. In the context of a sentence, the meaning is determined by pitch.

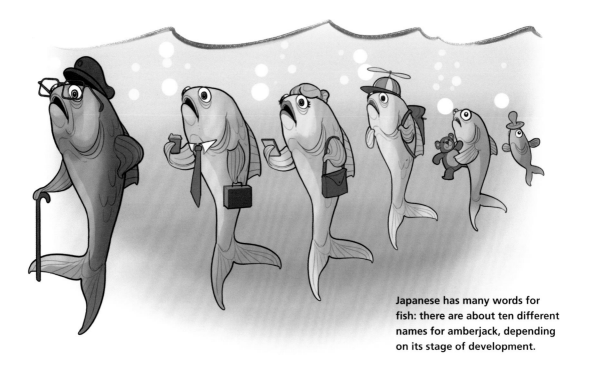

Japanese has many words for fish: there are about ten different names for amberjack, depending on its stage of development.

Vocabulary

Just as it is often said that Arabic has a lot of words for camels, Japanese similarly has a great many words for fish. These can denote not just different species but even different stages in growth of the same species. There are, for example, ten or so words for different sizes of the fish called in English amberjack. This might be considered natural for an island nation with a large culinary and economic interest in fishing.

The vocabulary of Japanese has been heavily influenced by Chinese. For example, the native Japanese word for *yesterday* is *kinoo*, but beside this there is *sakuzitu*, borrowed from Chinese. These borrowings are called *kango* (or *Han language*). They have the same kind of feel and prestige in Japanese as Latinate forms do in English next to their Anglo-Saxon equivalents (for example, *eat* vs. *consume*; *get* vs. *acquire*, and so on).

Politeness and honorifics

Japanese also distinguishes between words that it is proper only for men to use among themselves and equivalents that might be employed when speaking in mixed company, or by a woman when she is speaking. For example, *sushi* is thought crude as a word and if a man wants to mention the dish to a woman, he would say *o-sushi*. The prefix has the effect of rendering the word more polite.

This is in reality just one aspect of an elaborate system of politeness, deference and hierarchy that is encoded into the language at the level of both vocabulary and grammar. The so-called honorific forms are used when speaking directly to, or merely even about, a person to whom particular respect is felt to be due. The contrasting humble forms are used when speaking of oneself, or of a person in one's own group, when a contrast with the group of an exalted addressee is sought.

For example, if I am speaking of my colleague Mr Tanaka within my own company, I would simply refer to him as Tanaka. If I wanted to refer to someone of the same name but in the employment of an esteemed interlocutor outside my own group, I would add the honorific suffix and refer to him as Tanaka-san.

Language Families

Honorific forms and suffixes

-san: Mr/Ms

-kun: for talking down to an inferior

-shi: very polite form used chiefly in writing to someone you do not know

-sama : much more exalted version of -san

senpai: senior contemporaries at school, university

kohai: opposite of senpai, for younger contemporaries at university

sensei: professionals in medicine, law; politicians, grandees

This works at the lexical level, where entire verbs may be substituted for each other. The normal Japanese word for *to give* is *ageru*. But if someone wants to refer to a present given to him by his boss, he would use the honorific alternative *kudasaru*. If, on the other hand, the same person wanted to refer to something he had given to the boss, he would use the humble verb *sashiageru*.

There is a separate suffix in Japanese, *-masu*, that denotes polite usage. It might overlap with honorific usage, but its basic function is to indicate a more refined register of speech for the benefit of the listener. It is thus common in all forms of speech other than the most relaxed and familiar. In ordinary speech, unmarked for politeness, for "there is a book on the shelf" you might say:

tana	ni	hon	ga	aru
shelf	LOCATIV	book	SUBJECT	be

The word *ni* is a particle marking location, and *ga* marks the subject of the verb. If you wanted to make the sentence more formal and polite, you could change the last verb from *aru* to *arimasu*. This is what you would expect in a TV broadcast, for example.

You can also see from the above example that the verb is not inflected to mark the person doing it. In many languages (such as German, Latin, Greek or Spanish) the verb has an ending to show who is doing the action: *I, you, he*, and so on. In Japanese, the verb is inflected very subtly, but for different things. There are two regular classes of verb (the classification depends on their phonetic shapes) and one irregular class. Each of these classes has a basic "dictionary form" that ends in *-u*. For example, *kau* (Group I; *to buy*) and *taberu* (Group II; *to eat*). What if you want to say "Mr Tanaka buys a newspaper"? There is no need to alter the verb to show that the subject is "he"; that is inferred from the context. So you say, in the polite *-masu* form:

Tanaka-san	wa	shinbun	o	kaimasu
Tanaka-HONORIFIC	SUBJECT	newspaper	OBJECT	buy

Whereas many languages could make this sentence negative just by inserting a word like "not", Japanese requires a special inflection for negativity. You take the verb and change the suffix from *-masu* to *-masen*.

Languages of the Americas

Although North America is linguistically dominated by English, and South America by Spanish and Portuguese, this section is about the indigenous languages of that vast area from Arctic Alaska to Cape Horn.

It is likely that modern human beings evolved first of all in east Africa; thus it follows that the first humans to populate the Americas arrived there from elsewhere. One hypothesis has them coming on foot across the Bering Strait from northeast Asia during the last interglacial period, when it was still possible to cross by land between the two continents. The subject is controversial, and others think a more diffuse pattern involving people travelling by sea from the coasts of east Asia is more likely. But the point remains that there are evident links between the native inhabitants of the Americas and those of east Asia. The languages they brought with them can be arranged into three broad geographical classes: Eskimo-Aleut, Central American and South American.

Eskimo-Aleut languages

Eskimo-Aleut languages are spoken by perhaps 260,000 people in Alaska, northern Canada, Greenland and Russia. Eskimo and Aleut are related but different forms of speech. They probably represent the last wave of migration into North America from Asia. In terms of grammar, for example, Eskimo has ergativity (see page 93), whereas Aleut does not. In terms of phonetics, Aleut lacks the consonants /p/ and /b/ and the vowels /e/ and /o/; Eskimo has /p/ but not /b/ and also lacks /e/ and /o/. All languages of this type are remarkable for their extreme agglutination: you start with a root and add suffixes indicating all kinds of grammatical and lexical information, with the result that you can say in a single word what in other languages would require an entire sentence. You have seen how Turkish can do this if it wants, but Eskimo-Aleut is much more given to it. Some

Frances Densmore, the leading authority of her day on the songs, music and culture of American Indian tribes, uses a wax cylinder phonograph to record a member of the Blackfoot people in 1916.

linguists in the 20th century used to say that these languages have an enormous number of words for snow. This is true, up to a point. But the number was grossly exaggerated because people counted as different words for snow what were actually just different sentences that happened to mention snow with adjectival and other suffixes thrown in. Nowadays known as the Great Eskimo Vocabulary Hoax, this was a failure on the part of linguists to grasp how Inuit really works.

Athabaskan languages

If you move only slightly farther south, you start to encounter the Athabaskan (or Na-Dene) languages of Canada, such as Dena'ina. Speakers of these

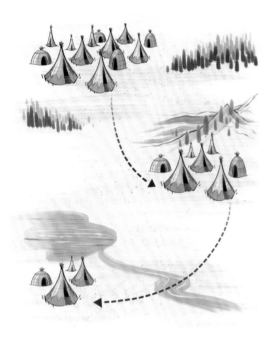

It is not unusal to find pockets of speakers of one language in separate areas, as smaller groups broke off from larger ones and settled elsewhere.

languages nowadays number only in the low thousands. They are also much farther south, in the form of Navajo and Apache. The map below shows their distribution as well as it can be reconstructed prior to encounters with incoming settlers. Such pockets of speakers in separate areas are not unusual: a group breaks off from the larger body but establishes itself only partially in ways that reflect the challenges of physical geography, the results of conquest and the difficulty of wresting a living from difficult territories. For example, some people might leave a large original group in Zone A in order to settle Zone B. The land is mountainous or there isn't enough water, so the breakaway group does not get properly established there. Having come too far to return to Zone A, some people move on to Zone C, leaving a pocket of speakers behind in Zone B. But then outsiders come onto the scene from elsewhere and kill many members of the group in Zone C, the survivors of which form another pocket of speakers.

There are in all perhaps 200 indigenous languages in North America, and their grouping

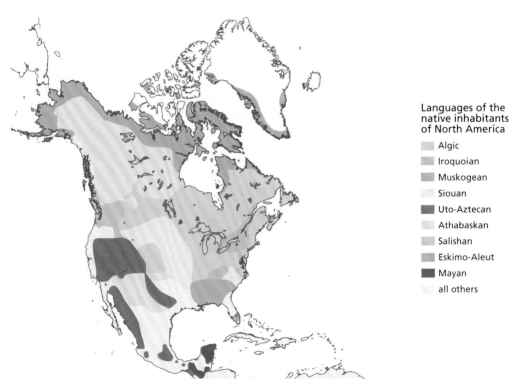

Languages of the native inhabitants of North America

- Algic
- Iroquoian
- Muskogean
- Siouan
- Uto-Aztecan
- Athabaskan
- Salishan
- Eskimo-Aleut
- Mayan
- all others

During the Second World War, the US Marine Corps recruited native speakers of languages such as Navajo, Sioux and Comanche to serve as code talkers (seen here are Henry Bake and George Kirk, in 1943). Due to the nature of their work, the contribution they made to the war effort was not widely known about until the 1990s.

into families is controversial. There were more than this, but the encroachment of English and Spanish has meant that many indigenous varieties of speech have died out. There is still a good deal of determination to preserve these languages by teaching them in schools. Perhaps the best known of them are Blackfoot, Cherokee, Cree, Navajo and Ojibwe.

Although the phonetics and grammar of these languages are interesting and important in themselves, they are perhaps best known to posterity for their use during the Second World War by the US Marines as a form of code. Navajo is the language most often mentioned in this context, although many other indigenous languages were so used. Because these languages are difficult and known to few living people outside the parts of America where they are spoken, it was relatively easy to find suitably qualified recruits. Their job did not depend simply on speaking to each other in Navajo in the hope that the enemy would not capture a speaker and so understand the signals. Instead, various common military terms were given equivalents in Navajo: thus a torpedo plane was a

tas-chizzi (*swallow*) in Navajo and a destroyer vessel was a *ca-lo* (*shark*). The code talkers memorized the codebooks so that they would not fall into enemy hands in the event that a soldier was captured. The code was remarkably quick to implement and was not broken by any opposing forces.

Central American languages

The languages of Central America are varied and complex. Nahuatl was the classical language of the Aztecs, attested from the time of the Spanish conquest in the 15th century. Descendants of it are spoken by some 1.5 million people in Mexico. The language has a complex phonetic structure. The sound [*tl*], for example, is actually a single articulation made in two different places simultaneously; it is not like the *-ul* heard in English *bottle*. There are no voiced stops (/b/, /d/, /g/), and no voiced aspirates.

Yucatec Maya is spoken in the Yucatán Peninsula by perhaps 800,000 people. One of its peculiar features is that it has glottalized ejective sounds. These also occur in the languages of the Caucasus (see page 93). Their existence in two such distant places is an interesting fact about language typology: two languages may share a rare feature like this, but there is such a thing as coincidence. Nobody would suggest a genetic relationship between them.

South American languages

South America presents many languages with a great deal of diversity (see map below).The single language with the most speakers is Quechua, spoken by some 9,000,000 people chiefly in Peru, Ecuador and Bolivia, but with scattered pockets elsewhere. Quechua is grammatically agglutinative like Turkish and others you have met in this section. There are plenty of markers for case and possession, but these are all bound morphemes added to words as a series of suffixes.

Like Quechua, Tariana (spoken on the Upper Amazon in Brazil) marks its verbs for evidentiality. Quechua has three and Tariana five different suffixes distinguishing between what is based on your own eyewitness evidence, what is based on other senses than sight, what is inferred from sensory evidence, what is assumed from broader criteria and what is reported. Imagine I want to say in Tariana that Maria made pumpkin soup. I could say this with five different suffixes on the verb meaning *to make*:

SUFFIX	MEANING
-ka	I actually saw Maria making soup from a pumpkin
-makha	I might not actually have seen her but I heard her using the liquidizer and clanking the pans and I smelled the familiar smell of pumpkin soup
-nikha	Even though I was out when the soup was made, I have come home and seen the pan in Maria's kitchen with the telltale traces of thick orange soup in the bottom
-sika	Everything has been tidied away and there is nothing to see in the kitchen but it is 2 November, O Dia dos Finados (All Souls' Day) in Brazil, and Maria always makes pumpkin soup on this day
-pidaka	I have not been anywhere near the house, but Manuel tells me that Maria made pumpkin soup

It is not that such distinctions are alien to other languages; the sentences on the right are proof of that. But very few languages have actually obligatory endings for them, forcing you to make a choice every time you speak.

Numerous indigenous languages are spoken in South America alongside the Spanish, Portuguese, Dutch, French and English introduced by European colonists.

Divided by a Common Language

Winston Churchill is supposed to have said that England and America were two countries divided by a common language. Whether it was actually said by him, Oscar Wilde or George Bernard Shaw does not really matter – there is some truth in it regardless.

The differences between British and American English are a perennial source of irritation or amusement to people on both sides of the Atlantic, and much of the irritation has historically been snobbery on the British side. A E Housman ticked off a correspondent for saying, "I have not got time to do this." This was, he thought, American, whereas a Brit would say, "I have not the time." That might have been true in the 1930s, but not today. The influence of America has undoubtedly proved too strong to resist.

What is worth remembering, though, is that American usage is not always new-fangled. In some respects it preserves historically correct forms that later British English has abandoned. Early settlers left England in the 17th century and took with them their own varieties of English. For example, *gotten* was regularly used at that time as the past participle of *to get*. Nowadays it sounds distinctly American, but it was not originally so. It is an exporting back to the UK of its own earlier speech; it was certainly not "made in the USA".

British vs. American English

In the same way, countless British people love to correct spelling in *-ize* words such as *organize*, believing that the proper English spelling is *-ise*. But as recently as the 1980s, *The Times* of London preferred the spelling *-ize*, and Oxford University Press still does, along with my own publisher's house style guide. People call it "the American spelling", but it is in reality nothing other than the older English spelling that people in the UK have progressively abandoned over the last half-century.

Other formations have been fashioned abroad and exported back to England; thus *sidewalk* for *pavement* represents an irreconcilable difference of usage. Where clothing is concerned, the differences can be rather serious: by *suspenders* an American means something men use to hold their trousers up, in England they are an item of lingerie.

A number of phonetic features are also noticeable. In England by the end of the 18th century, Londoners had stopped pronouncing /r/ after vowels – thus *pour* and *pore* sounded like

"A common language certainly makes an alliance easier; though you must not forget that it also makes quarreling easier," the Irish dramatist George Bernard Shaw (1856–1950) said in 1924.

By *pants* an American means something very different from an English person.

Excuse me. These were not the sort of pants I was asking for.

MEN'S CLOTHING

"We have really everything in common with America nowadays except, of course, language."

Oscar Wilde, The Canterville Ghost *(1887)*

paw, and still do in most varieties of English (except for Scotland and Ireland). The early British settlers of America left home before this change had occurred. Their speech was what linguists call rhotic and it was carried over into America. Over time, people in the southern and eastern states who kept up links with the Old Country came to imitate British speakers who had dropped the /r/. This kind of non-rhotic speech was felt by southerners to be prestigious. After the Civil War, and doubtless in reaction to it, people above the Mason-Dixon line began to restore rhoticity, which was not difficult because the written language had of course never dropped the historical /r/. Sociolinguistic studies show that it has for many decades increasingly been seen as a mark of high

social standing to have strongly audible post-vocalic /r/, for example fourth floo*r*.

Spanish and Portuguese

This phenomenon of division by a common language is not limited to English. It happens in any area where you have significant numbers of speakers of essentially the same language who have become separated by distance. Thus the Castilian Spanish of the Iberian Peninsula is different from the Spanish spoken in Latin America. In Spain, the /c/ in the ending of words like *distinción* is pronounced as a voiceless dental fricative, like the first sound in English *thing* (as opposed to *this*). It gives a characteristic lisping sound to such words. In South America, by

Some languages are spoken in multiple countries around the world. In each country, differences in pronunciation and vocabulary develop over time.

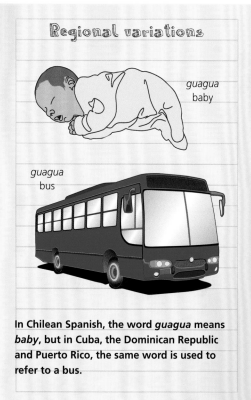

guagua
baby

guagua
bus

In Chilean Spanish, the word *guagua* means *baby*, but in Cuba, the Dominican Republic and Puerto Rico, the same word is used to refer to a bus.

contrast, it has come to be pronounced as [s]. At the level of vocabulary, a number of changes are evident. Castilian has *ordinador* for *computer*, from the same source as French *ordinateur*; in South America they say *computador*, surely under the influence of American English. The verb *coger* in Castilian means *to take* or *catch*; in Latin America it is a vulgar term for having sex. But Latin American Spanish is not always informal. Whereas Castilians use *vosotros* as a familiar plural pronoun to refer to a group of people they know, Latin Americans generally use *ustedes* (from *vuestras mercedes*, meaning *Your Graces*) with a third person plural verb. In Castilian Spanish, this is a mark of deferential politeness (like *Sie* as opposed to *ihr* in German); in Latin America it is just the normal plural form of address.

The Portuguese of Portugal is likewise different from that of Brazil. To some extent, this involves the same kind of changes in phonology that we have seen for Spanish. But there are also significant

Language Families

differences in vocabulary. A bus in Portugal is usually *ônibus*, whereas in Brazil it is *autocarro*. If something is brown, the Portuguese call it *marrom*, whereas in Brazil it is *castanho*.

French around the world

The French of France is different from that of Belgium. For example, French is well known for forming its numerals for 70, 80 and 90 by saying *soixante-dix* (60+10), *quatre-vingts* (4x20) and *quatre-vingt-dix* (4x20+10). In this system, 97 is *quatre-vingt-dix-sept* ((4x20)+10+7). In Belgian French, by contrast, they use the single words *septante* for 70 and *nonante* for 90. This seems very peculiar to people from France, but it makes 97 much easier to say: *nonante-sept*. A special case is made for 80: Belgium tends to agree with France in saying *quatre-vingts*. In Switzerland, by contrast, they say *huitante* (*huit* being the French for eight). In some regions of France, however, they say *octante*. This is based on *oct-*, which is from the same Latin root as *huit* but has not undergone as much phonetic evolution as *huit*.

There are also influences from Dutch. In Germanic languages generally there is a thing called the separable verb: for example, in Dutch a preposition like *mee* (*with*) can be prefixed to an infinitive like *komen* (*come*) so that *meekomen* means *go along with*. In a question, the preposition moves to the end of the sentence – thus in Belgian Dutch *gij komt mee?* means "are you coming with?" This has been taken over into French as *tu viens avec?* That sort of hanging preposition at the end of a sentence is no more normal in standard French than "are you coming with?" is in English. There are similar differences between the French of France and that of Quebec. For example, in Canada *espérer* can mean to *wait*; in standard French this sense is unknown, the meaning being *to hope*.

Varieties of German

The German spoken in Germany differs from that of Austria and Switzerland in accent and

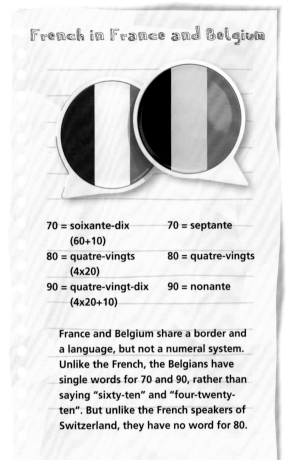

French in France and Belgium

70 = soixante-dix (60+10)	70 = septante
80 = quatre-vingts (4x20)	80 = quatre-vingts
90 = quatre-vingt-dix (4x20+10)	90 = nonante

France and Belgium share a border and a language, but not a numeral system. Unlike the French, the Belgians have single words for 70 and 90, rather than saying "sixty-ten" and "four-twenty-ten". But unlike the French speakers of Switzerland, they have no word for 80.

vocabulary. Such differences do not depend solely on distance between nations, as with Portugal and Brazil, but also on local identities among speech groups that are quite close together. The evening meal that the Germans usually call *Abendessen* (or *Abendbrot*) is generally called *Nachtmahl* in Austria and *Nachtessen* in Switzerland and parts of southern Germany. Cured knuckle of pork is called *Eisbein* in Germany, *Stelze* in Austria and *Wädli* in Switzerland.

These different features of English, Spanish, Portuguese, French and German are all equally valid. No one group owns these languages and the world is richer for the variations.

Writing Systems

Language is primarily a spoken phenomenon, as you can tell from the way it is often described with a word that means simply *tongue*, such as French *langue* or Greek *glossa*. Students of spoken language are called linguists; those who examine written language are philologists. The two disciplines go together – no philologist can get very far without a good grasp of linguistics, and only a small number of languages have no written tradition. But it is worth bearing in mind that writing is secondary because otherwise you can be led astray by oddities of spelling. The written record often preserves historical information about how the language was once pronounced. Spelling systems tend to be remarkably conservative.

But the subject of writing is compelling in itself. It is remarkable how many ways people have found to represent their speech, from pictures to alphabets. Whatever is chosen, there is generally a movement away from drawing the thing spoken of and toward more abstract representations of things and sounds. It is important, though, not to suppose that the whole history of writing is about the evolution toward alphabetic systems.

The Origins of Writing

Writing is everywhere, and we take it for granted. But the step taken by human beings when we started to make marks on stone and clay in order to record ideas and words was as revolutionary, in its own way, as the development of speech itself.

In the Lascaux Cave in southern France there are famous prehistoric wall paintings of wild animals that are some 17,000 years old. Some of them, you might say, tell a story: the hunt, the kill. But they are paintings, not writing. You might use them to tell a story, but these images do not represent actual spoken words.

Pictograms, logograms and ideograms

The earliest examples of what we might think of as writing come from the ancient Mesopotamian civilization in the southern part of modern Iraq and date from around 3500 BC. They are simple pictorial representations of the thing referred to, often with a numerical tally of how many such things were at issue. Historians believe that the language recorded in these texts was Sumerian.

A representation of a word through by means of drawing the thing in question is called a pictogram,

and remains with us today. When we visit a public lavatory, we will often see an image of a man or woman on the door but mentally we read *ladies* or *gentlemen*.

Still at a relatively early stage in history, scribes began to move away from pictographs toward logograms. Like a pictogram, a logogram originally evoked a single word but was more stylized, less immediately recognizable as a drawing of, say, an ox. The cartoon opposite shows this in the case of a bird: early pictograms looked like a bird, and a reader would have pronounced the Sumerian word for *bird*, which is *mushen*, when reading the sign aloud. But then the scribes turned the pictogram through 90 degrees and made it slightly more abstract. When the Mesopotamians started to write by impressing wedge-like symbols (cuneiform) into clay instead of scratching outlines, the symbols become yet more abstract. This development can already be seen by about 2500 BC. By 700 BC the

The walls of the Lascaux grotto in France are covered in paintings and engravings of animals, human figures and symbols that date back around 17,000 years.

This stone tablet with protocuneiform script dates from around 3200 BC. It was found at the site of the Mesopotamian city of Kish, in what is now Iraq.

3200 BC   3000 BC   2400 BC   1000 BC

Over the course of 2,000 years, the word *bird* evolved from a Sumerian pictograph through to an abstract, symbolic representation.

sign had lost all likeness to a bird and the reader simply had to learn that this particular sign meant *bird*; there was no way you could guess the meaning just by looking.

An even more abstract development is the ideogram, in which a symbol represents a word even though there is often little, if any, obvious connection between the symbol and the word. We are familiar with this from the modern world: the symbols &, £, $ and @ cut across all languages. The symbol for pound sterling is £, but very few people have it in mind that this is a stylized letter L and is short for Latin *librum*, meaning a pound in weight. The ampersand (&) is a highly stylized version of some handwritten forms of Latin *et*, meaning *and*. A German speaker who sees an ampersand will understand *und*, whereas a Spanish speaker will think *y*. The numerical system is the same: the symbols 1, 2, 3 were adopted from Arabic. They

The Narmer Palette, an Egyptian sculpture from c.2900 BC, contains very early examples of writing, in the form of the logograms above a scene that may depict the unification of upper and lower Egypt, c.3100 BC.

have no more intrinsic relation to the sounds *one*, *two*, *three* than to the words *eins*, *zwei*, *drei*. They are ideograms.

Hieroglyphics and the rebus principle

Writing in Egypt (hieroglyphs) got under way slightly later than in Mesopotamia; the earliest examples date from around 3000 BC. The Palette of Narmer (see page 131) dates from c.2900 BC. It consists mostly of pictures, but also shows a remarkable evolution (which also took place in Mesopotamia). In the top line of the front side of the palette is a box called a serekh (forerunner of the later cartouche, see page 157), in which Egyptologists expect to find a royal name. It contains, among other things, a pictograph denoting a catfish and the symbol for a chisel. The Egyptian for *catfish* is known from later sources to have been something like *na'r* and the

word for *chisel* was *mr*. So these symbols are not being used to refer to a fish and a tool: by virtue of their sounds, they are taken together to write the name of King Narmer.

This process is known as the rebus principle: a symbol that began life as a pure pictograph is used instead for its phonetic qualities. French speakers do something similar when they write *K7* to mean an audio or video cassette (K = *ka*, 7 = *sept*, so taken together sound like *cassette*). This step was very important in both cuneiform and hieroglyphic scripts because it meant that scribes could use a symbol to refer not only to the thing it depicted (which they did quite rarely), but also to other words that sounded the same or began with the same letter. A cuneiform sign that looked like a star was read *dingir* in Sumerian and meant *god*. The Akkadian equivalent was *ilum*: so when they saw the sign that Sumerians would have read as

Modern ideograms

Ideograms are abstract representations of words that are the same in every language – the ampersand symbol always means *and*, no matter which language you speak, and the dollar sign is understood around the world.

Writing Systems

dingir, Akkadians said *ilum*. They went even further than this and used it to represent the sounds *el* and *le* in words that had them on account of the presence of the *l* sound in both. They extended it to other sounds as well.

The Mesopotamian and Egyptian writing systems were thus able to become extremely subtle and flexible once the link was broken between a particular symbol and a particular word. But this

The sculptures and reliefs that decorated Assyrian palaces are awe-inspiring, but the greatest cultural legacy of ancient Mesopotamia is the written word.

also makes the texts very tricky to read: one single Akkadian sign that is usually read as *lum* could also, depending on context, be read as *hum*, *gum*, *lu*, *num*, *kus* or *hus*! There is little wonder that scribes in Egypt and Mesopotamia were an elite class.

"Emojis are by no means taking away from our written language but rather accentuating it by providing a tone that words on their own often cannot. They are, in a sense, the most evolved form of punctuation we have at our disposal."

Emmy J. Favilla, A World Without "Whom":
The Essential Guide to Language in the Buzzfeed Age

Cuneiform and Hieroglyphs

Mesopotamian cuneiform and Egyptian hieroglyphs, the earliest forms of writing, began with pictograms. These are handy if all you want to do is keep a numerical tally of some easily recognizable animal; they are less useful for expressing abstract ideas.

At the time we are talking about (c.3500 BC), human language was fully developed. There was plenty to talk about, but the means of recording speech did not exist. This seems hard to imagine now. But not everyone had the same anxieties that we do about keeping records. In many traditional cultures even today, the telling of stories from memory is valued more highly than the solitary reading of books. It is striking that the earliest examples of writing had little to do with creative arts and more to do with assisting nascent bureaucracies to keep records.

Early Sumerian writing

So how was the pictographic script of the Sumerians adapted to record the subtleties of

The earliest examples of writing focus on basic administration: this tablet bears a record of barley distribution, with symbols of men, dogs and boars.

the spoken word? A number of approaches were adopted simultaneously. First, a sign could be used as a logogram to indicate a whole word. The Sumerian sign below meant *mouth*, and was pronounced *ka*:

By a natural enough extension, this sign also came to be used for related concepts, even though the Sumerian words for these were actually not *ka* but something quite different. Thus it came to mean *inim* (*word*), *zu* (*tooth*), *dug* (*to speak*) and *gu* (*to shout*).

Secondly, a Sumerian sign might be used as a syllabogram, to indicate not a word but a syllable, or part of one. For example, the sign below was pronounced *ba* and meant *to give*:

But it also served to write the syllable *ba-*, for example as a prefix in certain verb forms. In developed Sumerian writing these grammatical affixes were written using syllabograms, whereas the verbal root itself would be written using an ideogram. This is reminiscent of the system used in Japanese, in which content words such as verbs and nouns are generally written with ideographs called *kanji* (taken from Chinese but pronounced with Japanese phonetic values; see page 151), whereas any inflectional markers are written using syllabic characters called *hiragana* (see page 152).

Thirdly, many words were preceded or followed by a sign that itself meant something, but was used in writing only to indicate the class to which another

This ancient Sumerian relief includes elements of pictographic script.

word belonged. For example, the name of the god Enlil was written with the syllabic signs below:

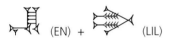 (EN) + (LIL)

However, it would also have the following sign for AN or DINGIR, both meaning *god* in Sumerian, prefixed to it to make clear that the name was that of a god.

What was written is transcribed as ᵈEN.LIL but the determinative sign ᵈ⁽ⁱⁿᵍⁱʳ⁾ was not pronounced in speech, where the word was just *Enlil*. The names of cities were generally followed by the sign KI, meaning *place*:

Thus UNUGᵏⁱ is read without pronouncing the *ki* and indicates "the city of Uruk".

Akkadian writing

Sumerian died out as a spoken language around 2000 BC, but the signs it used were adopted by speakers of a Semitic language generally known as Akkadian, whose northern variety is often called Assyrian, and the southern, Babylonian. The phonemic repertory and syllable structure of Akkadian were not the same as those of Sumerian. In particular, there was no equivalent in Sumerian of the so-called emphatic consonants in Akkadian, varieties of /t/, /s/ and /k/ that were pronounced with the body of the tongue broad and low in the mouth and its root drawn back so as to occlude the pharynx. Whereas Akkadian had fricative *s, ś, š, s, z, ḫ*, Sumerian had only *z, s*, and *š*. All of this meant that some ambiguities were bound to result.

The overall method was more or less like that used in written Sumerian: any given sign might represent a word or a syllable (or part of one) or a determinative. But the situation was complicated by the fact that Sumerian, although no longer a living language, exerted an enormous influence as the language of religion and learning. Scribes knew it and were apt to use Sumerian logograms to write Akkadian words that, nevertheless, were read in Akkadian with their Akkadian values (rather as Japanese scribes used Chinese ideograms). Such writings are called Sumerograms.

For example, you have already met the Sumerian sign pronounced *ba* and meaning *to give*. In Akkadian, this sign evolved to be written in a different form:

 (Sumerian)   ⊢⊣ (Akkadian)

It was pronounced quite differently as *qiāšum*, though, because that was the Akkadian for *to give*. It could also be used to write the syllable *ba* and even *pa*, with the first sound devoiced. This was quite a serious problem because the difference between voiced and voiceless sounds is phonemic in Akkadian, yet this distinction is not made in the writing system for many syllables of the shape VC or CV.

Broadly speaking, it is the syllabic use of the sounds that is most complex in Akkadian. It is fortunate that these syllabic spellings are found because otherwise we would have little clue as to the pronunciation in Akkadian of many Sumerograms. Scribes at various periods went to great efforts to produce word lists that spelled out obscure or difficult logograms. But even these

syllabic signs were polyvalent: the sign below could be read *tar*, *kud*, *has*, *sil* or *gug*.

The converse is also found: a single syllabic sound might be written using numerous different signs. The sound *sa*, for example, might be written with at least 11 different signs.

This might seem like a recipe for confusion, but the system lasted for about 3,000 years and was even adapted by other cultures to write their own languages – including the quite unrelated Hittite. One great strength of the system was that the use of ideograms made it compact – it was not necessary to spell everything out syllabically. And, although the variations described above exist, it has to be said that the scribes working at any given place or time tended to limit the number of values they attributed to this or that sign, rarely exceeding three.

The hieroglyphic writing system

Egyptian hieroglyphs have in common with Mesopotamian cuneiform the fact that they began life as pictograms. Cuneiform signs, however, very soon became stylized and unrecognizable as

The role of scribes in Egypt

Like cuneiform, hieroglyphs are a subtle and complicated writing system. In ancient Egypt, training as a scribe offered young men a way of moving up the social ranks by allowing them to take up high-status administrative positions.

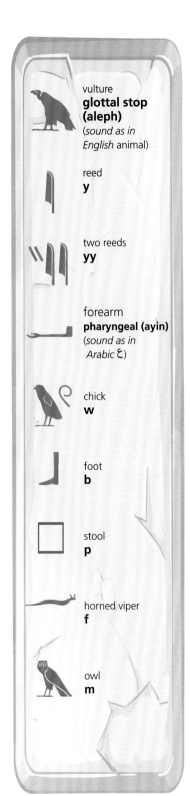

vulture
glottal stop (aleph)
(*sound as in English* animal)

reed
y

two reeds
yy

forearm
pharyngeal (ayin)
(*sound as in Arabic* ﻉ)

chick
w

foot
b

stool
p

horned viper
f

owl
m

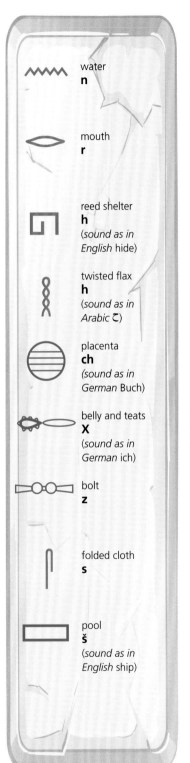

water
n

mouth
r

reed shelter
h
(*sound as in English* hide)

twisted flax
h
(*sound as in Arabic* ﺡ)

placenta
ch
(*sound as in German* Buch)

belly and teats
X
(*sound as in German* ich)

bolt
z

folded cloth
s

pool
š
(*sound as in English* ship)

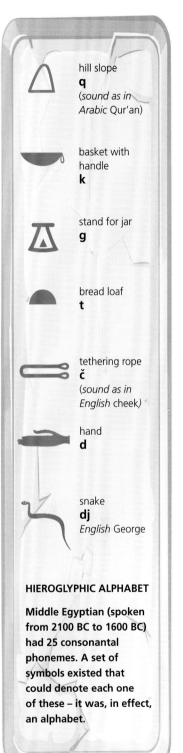

hill slope
q
(*sound as in Arabic* Qur'an)

basket with handle
k

stand for jar
g

bread loaf
t

tethering rope
č
(*sound as in English* cheek)

hand
d

snake
dj
English George

HIEROGLYPHIC ALPHABET

Middle Egyptian (spoken from 2100 BC to 1600 BC) had 25 consonantal phonemes. A set of symbols existed that could denote each one of these – it was, in effect, an alphabet.

This Egyptian papyrus dating from c.1330 BC shows the Pharaoh Tutankhamun and Osiris, the god of the dead, his wife Isis and the goddess Hathor.

drawings because scribes had taken to making them not with a stylus, but with the triangular end of a cut reed impressed into clay. This never happened to hieroglyphs. Although cursive writing had been invented, workmen continued to carve fully pictorial, non-stylized hieroglyphs into stone and scribes preserved the original forms in writing. This does not mean that hieroglyphs remained simply pictographic; some ideographic writings did persist, but the system also went down the path of assigning phonetic values to certain signs.

Middle Egyptian (the classical phase of the language spoken from 2100 BC to 1600 BC) had 25 consonantal phonemes. A set of symbols existed that could denote each one of these – it was, in effect, an alphabet. It is commonly found in reference books and is often used for activities of the "Write your name in Ancient Egyptian" kind (see page 137).

But the Egyptians did not actually write their language like this. They used a combination of these signs and others that had a phonetic or logographic character together with some that were purely pictographic and served to show the general category to which the preceding word belonged (man, woman, god and so on). From about 3000 BC to 2000 BC, there were some 1,000

characters; during the next millennium, the number settled to about 750; toward the end of the 1st millennium BC the number rose sharply into the low thousands.

In addition to uniliteral signs, there were signs that could write two or three phonemes depending on what was required. For example, this sign representing a desert hare wrote the sequence *wn*:

And this sign, the black ibis, was used to write *gm*:

Triliterals were also found, such as this one, which was pronounced *hnm*:

The derivation of these signs is often by phonetic association. In the case of the black ibis, its Egyptian name was *gmt*. By taking the first two sounds, a convenient way of writing any instance of *gm* was created.

You can see straightaway that some of these words look impossible to pronounce. This is because the hieroglyphic writing system, in common with that of other Afro-Asiatic languages, did not write vowels. This might seem odd, but the same is true of Arabic, Hebrew and many other scripts. But whereas Classical Hebrew, for example, had a continuous reading tradition for religious purposes long after it ceased to be a spoken language, Ancient Egyptian did not. When it died out, the secret of reading it was lost for nearly two millennia. And although the consonants have been more or less securely established, the vowels are largely irrecoverable – although some help comes from Coptic, the final stage of the Egyptian language, which is preserved in the religious liturgy of Coptic Christians. Standard practice has generally been to insert an /e/ vowel as necessary except, where 𓄿 or ⌢ occur, when /a/ is written instead. Thus the following sequence

Writing Systems

In ancient Egypt, only a small proportion of people were literate, and scribes played a vital role in the kingdom.

is transliterated *wbn r′ m pt* but pronounced something like *weben ra em pet*:

You can see that there are not just uniliteral symbols here. *Wbn* is written as chick (*w*) + foot (*b*) + water (*n*). But the circular sign below is the sun, written because *to rise* has to do with the sun, and the determinative makes this clear. A homophonous Egyptian word *weben* means *overflow* and is written with the same three uniliteral signs, but the determinative for *overflow* would not be the sun but a heap of corn: △. This resolves any ambiguity. *Ra* (the name of the sun)

has the same determinative. *Em* (*in*) is written and needs no other determinative because it is a preposition whose meaning is plain. Finally, *pet* (*sky*) is written with the symbols for *p* and *t* and also with a logogram that is meant to depict the overarching vault of heaven:.

In this particular example, the text is read from left to right. You can tell this because the animals are all facing to the left and the rule is that you read into their faces. The whole text could be made to face the other way, and then it would be read from right to left. Egyptian scribes had considerable freedom over this. They also placed the characters on top of each other if it was more aesthetically pleasing than putting them one after another in a straight line.

Syllabic Writing

Cuneiform and hieroglyphic writing are complex mixtures of strategies: some signs are ideograms, others logograms or syllabograms, and yet others represent single phonemes. There are alternatives, however.

A **syllabary** is made up of symbols, each of which denotes a single syllable, usually of the shape CV (consonant–vowel), but possibly also V or CVC.

Linear B and Amharic

Perhaps the best-known example of syllabic writing is the Linear B system, which was used by the inhabitants of Bronze Age Greece and the surrounding islands to write an early form of Greek on clay tablets. It has many logograms too, but this does not alter the fundamentally syllabic nature of the script.

The characteristic thing about a syllabary is that, for any given consonant (C), there is a series of symbols to represent the sequence C*a*, C*e*, C*i*, C*o*, C*u* but the signs used for any modification of a given C bear no relation to each other. You could not guess from the sign ⵣ (*sa*) that it begins with

the same sound as ⵗ (*se*); or by looking at the sign ⵏ (*re*) that it ends with the same sound as the sign ⊜ (*qe*).

Linear B was borrowed from a culture whose language was not related to Greek. This is evident from the problems of writing. Linear B has symbols for V or CV, but Greek syllables can also take the form CVC. The Greek *ekʰontes* (masculine plural) means *having*: in Linear B it is written as *e-ko-te*. The aspirate /kʰ/ is written as though it were simply /k/; the -*nt*- cluster is not written because you can only write CV, not CVC; the final -*s* is not written either as the script again does not allow for it. As most of the grammatical information in a Greek word is encoded by the endings, it is not helpful to have a script that suppresses many of them.

People sometimes use the term "syllabary" to describe the writing system of the Amharic

Knossos, the ancient capital of Crete, was the centre of the Minoan civilization, which flourished from about 300 BC to about 1100 BC.

This Minoan tablet with Linear B script is dated to 1400 BC. The Minoan civilization is named after Minos, a ruler from Greek legend.

language of Ethiopia, but it is in fact quite different. There is a basic form in each series that represents a given consonant followed by the short vowel [ə]. Any change in vowel is accomplished by making a subtle modification to identify the vowel. Look at this table comparing the *b-* and *s-* series:

	-ə	**-u**	**-i**	**-a**	**-e**
b-	በ	ቡ	ቢ	ባ	ቤ
s-	ሰ	ሱ	ሲ	ሳ	ሴ

You can see at once that the signs all resemble each other. Even if you did not know their value, you could guess that they were all related.

The same is true for the vowel sounds: you can look at any sign and more or less tell from the modification which vowel is being written. Looking at the table above, you can see that the sound /e/ is marked by a closed loop at the bottom right of any character. If we look at how /e/ is applied to some other consonant signs, it clearly follows through quite systematically:

	-e
h-	ሄ
l-	ሌ
m-	ሜ
r-	ሬ
t-	ቴ

A system of this sort is called an alpha-syllabary or abugida to differentiate it from a pure syllabary, in which characters encoding similar consonants or vowels bear no resemblance to each other.

The Devanagari system

The Devanagari system used to write Sanskrit and many of the modern languages of India works in the same way. Look at the sequence below:

त	ता	ति	ती	तु	तू
ta	ta	ti	ti	tu	tu

तृ	तॄ	तॢ	तॣ	ते	तै	तो	तौ
tr	tr	tl	tl	te	tai	to	tau

The basic shape of the character for *t-* is apparent in the first form, used to write *ta*. To indicate *t-* followed by any other vowel, modifications are made using various vowel symbols. These are stable throughout the Devanagari system and will have the same meaning when applied to any other consonantal sign.

The Alphabet

Like the symbols of a syllabary, alphabetic characters represent the sounds of a language, but this writing system requires fewer different characters.

You have seen so far examples of writing based on pictograms, logograms or syllabograms, and sometimes a mixture of all of these in one system. An alphabet is something different again: this writing system involves having consonants and vowels represented separately.

Early alphabetic writing

Various marks that appear to be early attempts at alphabetic writing have been found in the plain of Moab, Israel, and are dated to c.2500–1800 BC. They cannot be readily interpreted. The earliest intelligible alphabetic writing comes from inscriptions bearing the name of King Shaphatbaal of Byblos (Jubeil in modern Lebanon) and dates to not before 1500 BC. Approximately contemporary with this is a fragment of pottery excavated at Lachish, a major city of ancient Judah (in modern Israel). It dates from c.1400 BC and contains just two well-preserved letters and one damaged one. Nevertheless, on the basis of its similarity to later writing, it can be read as the Semitic name *bl'*, known from the Hebrew Bible in the form *Bela'*.

The origins of Phoenician script

It was from about 1200 BC that the Phoenician script came to prominence. This can be read securely and is recognizably the precursor of the familiar Classical Hebrew alphabet.

The origins of this form of writing are much debated and no firm conclusions are possible. Most historians are agreed that one possible precursor, Mesopotamian cuneiform, was not the origin of later Semitic alphabetic writing – there are some apparent similarities, but they are limited to one or two forms and an absence of correspondence

for the rest is not encouraging. The same is true if you compare Phoenician scripts directly with Egyptian hieroglyphs. That said, the so-called Sinaitic script, found in inscriptions dated to the 19th century BC in the Sinai Peninsula, is very suggestive. Many of the letter forms are extremely close to uniliteral hieroglyphs, as you can see from the diagram below; the problem is that there is little correspondence in sound. For example, the wavy line that writes /n/ in Egyptian is used to write /m/ in Proto-Sinaitic and the eye that writes /r/ in Egyptian writes a pharyngealized stop (Hebrew *ayin*) in Proto-Sinaitic. So although this script does not represent the missing link, direct influence seems undeniable.

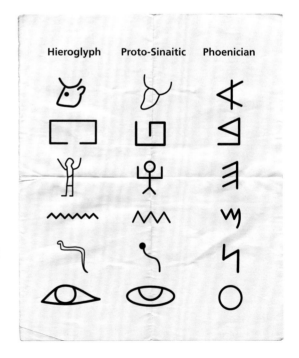

Hieroglyph	Proto-Sinaitic	Phoenician

Writing Systems

Alphabet or abjad?

According to the definition given at the start, however, none of this Semitic writing is an alphabet in the true sense because it does not mark the vowels. To this day, books and newspapers in Arabic and Hebrew script do not mark the vowels. The Arabic *qatala* means *he killed*, whereas *qutila* means *he was killed*. The difference is pretty fundamental and depends entirely on the vowels. But these are not routinely written: both would appear as قتل (*qtl*). Speakers of the language are supposed not to need help; such ambiguities are expected to be resolved by looking at the context. This is all very well in theory. In practice, the shorter the text, the greater the likelihood of misunderstanding.

The only place where vowels are routinely written is in printed editions of the Hebrew Bible or the Qur'an. There is a long so-called "reading tradition", which required the correct pronunciation of these sacred texts, so great effort was made to record the vowels for this reason. But their writing is done by means of marks under or

over or after the letters in question and we can see from the historical record that these were late in developing and were plainly not part of the script as it originally developed.

If a system of writing is close to being alphabetic but does not mark the vowels, as with Arabic and Hebrew, it is technically called not an alphabet but an abjad. The first true alphabet came about when the early Greeks borrowed the Phoenician letters and used it to write their own language. In the process, they assigned letters for the vowels. This did not happen in the way that might seem most obvious to us with hindsight. The Phoenician I looks more like what Westerners think of as a capital I, but Phoenicians used it for /z/ and so did the Greeks, since they had that sound in their own language. The Phoenician ∿ wrote a consonantal /y/ sound but the Greeks adapted it for a vocalic /i/.

The Classical Roman alphabet consisted of 23 letters – J, U and W are medieval additions.

The Roman alphabet

The inhabitants of Italy in the middle of the 1st millennium BC adopted one local version of this alphabet from the Greeks and adapted it to write Etruscan, Latin and other languages of Italy. Thus the so-called Roman alphabet was born, which is used in so many languages today.

The various languages written in Roman script are not necessarily any better adapted to it than Greek was to Phoenician or Latin was to Greek. Some alterations are usually necessary. Sometimes this is as simple – if confusing – as assigning a different value to the letter. Thus an English and German speaker might both write *W*, but each refers to a quite different sound. The same is true of *V*, which Germans use to write what English speakers generally write with *F*. That is not the end of the process. In French and German, a lot of differences in vowel sounds need to be marked; this is often done by putting accents or dots over the letters in question, thereby avoiding the need for a separate letter altogether. With Polish and several other languages, however, modifications such as ł are needed; these were originally intended to distinguish between the so-called dark and clear

In French, the acute accent (as in *café*) and grave accent (as in *père*, meaning *father*) are used to change the sound of the letter *e*.

varieties of /l/, and the former of which has now come close to an English /w/.

When you start to learn a foreign language, you will often be told by your teacher that, whereas the writing system of your own language is illogical and confusing, the writing system of the language

Writing Systems

> **"This invention of yours will produce forgetfulness in the souls of those who have learned it because they will stop exercising their memories. Putting their trust in writing, they will be reminded of things from the outside by the use of external symbols rather than remembering them from the inside by themselves. You have discovered a charm not of remembering but of reminding."**
>
> *Plato,* Phaedrus, *section 275a*

you are learning is the most perfect ever invented. These claims are frequently made for German, Italian and Sanskrit. English spelling is undoubtedly among the most confusing in the world for learners because of its historical conservatism, often preserving pronunciations from centuries ago or etymological features that few living speakers know or care about. But anyone who spends much time learning another language soon learns that the spelling systems they use have their own confusing quirks and, to adapt a term from computing, What You See Is NOT What You Get.

The Cyrillic alphabet

The Russian alphabet was adapted in part from the Greek alphabet and is called Cyrillic in honour of St Cyril, who, with his brother St Methodius, brought Christianity to the Slavs. In fact, the earliest Cyrillic script developed around AD 900, by which time Cyril and his brother had been dead for decades. What they invented is nowadays called the Glagolitic script. It has some features that are recognizably borrowed from Byzantine Greek or other sources, but a lot of it appears to have been made up by them on the spot. This is not uncommon for missionaries, who are eager to get on with spreading the word and need a ready-made alphabet to do so. A number of alphabets invented for African languages are the result of efforts by missionaries, for example the script created by Samuel Crowther for Yoruba (but no longer used).

Rescued from slave traders as a child, Samuel Ajayi Crowther (c.1809–91) was the first African to be ordained by the Church Missionary Society in England.

The alphabet has greatly helped in the spread of literacy. Because it is so much easier to master than logographic systems or syllabaries, it allows writing to spread beyond a narrow class of educated scribes.

Writing Chinese

China evolved a very different strategy for writing from the alphabetic system used in the languages of Europe.

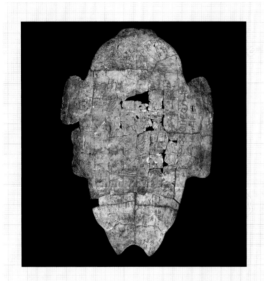

Around 1300–1050 BC in Henan province, writing was carved into this turtle shell to divine the outcome of a military campaign.

The first undoubted instances of Chinese writing date from c.1200 BC and were found near modern Anyang in eastern central China (see right). These texts were cut into ox bones and the shells of turtles and came into being as part of an oracular practice that involved incising questions to the gods onto these materials and putting them into fire. The material would crack in the heat and people thought they could read the answers to their questions by studying the patterns in these cracks. It is pure luck that any have survived at all.

People began to dig up oracle bones in the 19th century, unaware of the artifacts' historical significance. They soon became incorporated as

an ingredient in various forms of traditional Chinese medicine. This involved grinding up the bones and shells and giving them to patients to ingest, and would probably have resulted in the loss of the entire body of early Chinese writing had not a civil servant with an interest in palaeography called Wang Yirong (1845–1900) contracted malaria and been prescribed some of these bones as a treatment. It is said that he was the first to appreciate their true importance.

These early characters were to some extent pictographic, like the early writing of Egypt and Mesopotamia. The sign 𝍀, for example, appears to have represented rain, and the sign 𝅘 to have denoted the moon.

In the absence of a detailed drawing, though, the pictograms are never more than a stylized representation. The reader has to know that 𝅘 represents the moon rather than perhaps an ear or an eye. As it happens, the sign for ear is 𝅘 and for eye is 𝆄. The point is that you have to know the

Writing Systems

system to know this; you cannot just look at one of these signs and be sure what it is supposed to represent.

In any event, the system would never get very far if it depended purely on pictograms. As in Egypt and Mesopotamia, so in China we find that the signs become stylized and bear little relation to anything in nature. Thus, although the early sign for water was 川, it had evolved to 水 by the 3rd century BC.

The Chinese then took a critically important step that had already been taken by the Sumerians and Egyptians: they began to use symbols not because of what they looked like, but because of phonetic associations. For example, the character 又 originally denoted the hand and was pronounced *yòu*. But the word *yòu* also meant (and still means) *again*. So by association of sound, the sign 又 could be used to write *yòu* (*again*). In today's Chinese, however, the word for *hand* is *shǒu* and is written with the symbol 手.

Characters and radicals

Modern Mandarin Chinese (spoken as a first language by perhaps 70 percent of the population) has a somewhat restricted range of permitted forms that a syllable can take. There are about 400 possible syllables, compared with many thousands in English. But as you have seen (see Chinese, page 115), Chinese is a tonal language. The word *zhū* (tone 1) can mean *red* and is pronounced quite differently from *zhú* (tone 2) meaning *bamboo*; *zhǔ* (tone 3) means *master*, whereas *zhù* (tone 4) means *pillar*. This means that you can have a much larger number of words, especially when you take into account that, within a single tone, you can have lots of different words that are pronounced the same. Thus *pillar* is only one possible meaning of *zhù* (tone 4); it can also mean *to bore through*, *to build*, *to cast* (of metals), *to express good wishes*, *to help*, *to pour*, *to stay* or *to write*.

This means that the spoken language is formidably complex. Not only must a person be able to differentiate between tones properly (and more tones are recognized in some parts of China than in others), she must also know the full range of homophones (see page 115) within any given tone. Usually, of course, context will assist in narrowing down the possibilities to the correct one.

How does the writing system deal with this? In theory, it could simply assign a character to every different concept in the language and have no regard to sound. But as we have seen already, this

Speaking Chinese involves being able to differentiate a subtle range of tones. It is perhaps not surprising that people who speak a tonal language are more likely to have perfect pitch.

I wasn't asking you to help build my new extension! I said you're welcome to stay in it!

is not quite how it works. The script does have regard to words that sound the same or similar.

Let us go back to the example of *zhū* given on page 147, which means, among other things, *red*. When it means this, it is written 朱. But there is another meaning of *zhū* (tone 1), and that is *pearl*. This is written 珠. You can see at once that the right-hand side of both characters looks the same. This is not because pearls are thought to be red; it is simply that the two words are pronounced in the same way and the script takes this into account.

The added element on the left is called a radical. There are about 230 of these in Chinese and they serve to indicate the sort of thing that a composite character like 珠 denotes. A reader who knows the language might spot that it is going to be something pronounced *zhū* (tone 1) because that is what the right-hand section of the character is.

A Chinese typewriter has a bed of 3,000 common characters, which the typist selects with a lever. Additional characters can be swapped in as needed.

The left-hand section, in this case, is a word that can stand by itself to mean *jade*. But when used as a radical, it tells you that the thing referred to is a precious stone, so the reader thinks: "Sounds like *zhū* and is a precious stone – ah, yes! Not *red*, not *pig*, but *pearl*". It is important to realize, though, that unless you know that the word for *red* is written as it is and sounds as it does, and that the radical for *jade* also indicates precious stones in general, the way in which the word for *pearl* is written will not help you.

Reproducing Chinese characters

Chinese characters were traditionally drawn using a brush and, as you can see, are made up of separate strokes. Some characters may be made up of as many as 25 strokes. This calls for considerable skills in memorizing and recognizing them. You can also imagine, before the advent of the computer, what a nightmare it was to make typewriters. How do you design a machine that can produce one of potentially thousands of characters that you might

Writing Systems

One of the most complex Chinese characters in contemporary usage is *biáng* – it takes 57 brush strokes to complete in its traditional form (it only takes 43 strokes in simplified Chinese). The photograph shows a contestant writing this character as part of a competion held in Xi'an, the capital of Shaanxi province in northwest China, in which almost 2,000 local calligraphers took part. The character is used in the name of a type of noodle that is popular in this part of the country.

need? The answer was something much more like the sort of apparatus used by a printer, with each character on a separate metal block that was selected using a special picking system.

If the problem of typing went away with the computer, the problem of literacy did not. Literacy levels in China are high at about 91 percent, but that has been achieved by a considerable simplification of the script during the 1950s. A character such as 麵 (*miàn*) means *noodle* and had 22 strokes! It was simplified to 面, which has only 9, and makes it much easier to read. The problem comes if you want to read anything written before the 1950s. In practice, if you want to do that you have to learn the old system as well. That is the problem with all spelling reforms: they involve setting the past to one side.

Calligraphic strokes

The Chinese character for "forever", above, uses a wide variety of strokes. Two or more basic strokes can be combined to make a compound stroke.

Writing Japanese

Chinese and Japanese could scarcely be more different in structure, sound and vocabulary. But they look quite similar if you just glance at a text in either language.

To the untrained eye, the likeness is easy to see; the differences are harder to spot. Alongside complex symbols like 獅子 (*lion*) in a Japanese text you find simpler forms like く, which spells the syllable *ku*. This is typical of the whole system. It is quite similar to Mesopotamian writing in that it is a combination of logograms and syllabograms (see Cuneiform and Hieroglyphs, page 134).

Origins of Japanese writing

The logograms are fundamentally Chinese in origin; most of the syllabograms are also drawn from Chinese characters but are usually altered beyond recognition. That Japan should have borrowed from China is not surprising, given the long history of writing in China and its enormous influence during all periods. Chinese coins with writing dating from the first few centuries AD have been found in Japan. Mentions in later historical records suggest that the earliest Japanese use of writing for a large-scale work was in the *Sangyō gisho* (Commentaries on Three Buddhist Sutras), which dates from about AD 620. But that is known to us only from histories; the actual texts do not survive. The earliest Japanese writing to have survived to the present day is a manuscript of the *Kojiki*, a set of historical chronicles composed in the 8th century AD; the manuscript itself is a copy dating from AD 1372 (see opposite).

What can be gathered from these early sources is that books written in Chinese (for example, the works of Confucius in ten volumes) were passing via Korea to Japan by way of gifts between grandees. Speakers of Japanese had, at this stage, no indigenous writing system, so they adapted the Chinese. This is not surprising or unusual: speakers

Chinese vs Japanese

Chinese

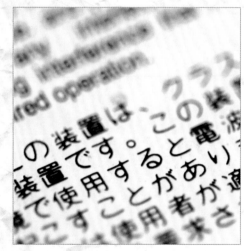

Japanese

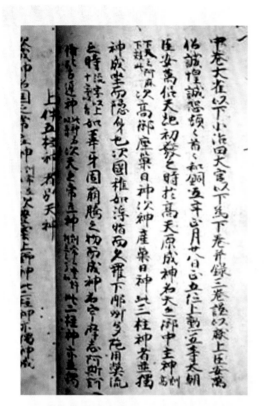

The oldest book in Japanese is *Kojiki*, or "Records of Ancient Matters". A collection of myths, events and traditions, it was written in AD 712 using Chinese characters to represent the sounds of Japanese. The oldest surviving copy, shown above, dates from AD 1371–2.

of Akkadian adapted the fundamentally unsuited Sumerian system to write their Semitic language, and speakers of Greek adapted the equally awkward Phoenician alphabet for their purposes.

Kanji

The earliest Japanese texts were written down solely in Chinese characters. These are known as *kanji*, which literally means *Han* ("Chinese") *letter*. Imagine you wanted to write the word for *sea*. The indigenous word in modern Japanese is *umi*, but you would write it using the Chinese character for *sea*, which is 海. In modern Chinese, this word is pronounced *hǎi* (in tone 3). Around the 8th or 9th

centuries AD, it was probably pronounced more like *kai*. A Japanese person seeing this character could pronounce it *kai* or *umi*.

This is still the case today: the Chinese language has effectively lent to Japanese a series of now-archaic pronunciations that persist in certain contexts. These so-called Sino-Japanese elements are also called by the generic name *onyomi*, which means *Chinese reading*. The pronunciation *umi* is known as *kunyomi* (*Japanese reading*).

There is no hard-and-fast rule to tell a reader when to use the *on* reading and when to use the *kun*. This makes the situation very complicated. But a rule of thumb is that if a *kanji* is found by itself, it is generally given the *kun* reading. If it is part of a compound word with other *kanji*, it generally has the *on* reading. Thus 海 by itself is pronounced *umi*, but when found as part of the sequence 大海 it is pronounced *kai* and the overall sequence is pronounced *taikai*, meaning *high sea*. A Chinese person might guess the meaning of this as well, since the Chinese character 天 (*tài*) is an adverb meaning *too much*.

The oddity of this situation takes a moment to grasp. These two languages are totally unrelated. The Chinese characters represented for the most part individual words such as noun and verbs. Japanese had nouns and verbs, of course, but their

Japanese *kanji* can either be read in the archaic Chinese way (*onyomi*) or the Japanese way (*kunyomi*).

structure was quite different from Chinese. For one thing, Japanese has more open than closed syllables – in other words, more syllables that end in a vowel. Chinese was and is quite different, with many syllables ending in consonants. It soon became necessary to modify the Chinese characters in order to write foreign words and non-indigenous technical terms in, for example, Buddhist scriptures originally written in Sanskrit. There was also the fact that, in addition to nouns and verbs, Japanese has a rich array of so-called sentence particles. For example, -wa is used to indicate the topic of a sentence, to show that the thing before -wa is what we are meant to be focusing on.

One way in which this borrowing was done was to pretend that parts of the Chinese syllable did not exist. For example, the Chinese 天 was pronounced t'ien, but in Japanese the -n was

This print shows Murasaki Shikibu (c.978–1014), a lady-in-waiting at the Imperial court in the Heian period, writing *The Tale of Genji*. This court romance is sometimes considered to be the world's first novel.

ignored and the character was used to write the syllable *te* where it was needed.

Katakana and hiragana

That method was never going to be entirely satisfactory, however, and so, beginning around the 9th century AD, a separate method was used far more extensively. More often than not, this involved starting with a Chinese character whose sound you wanted to imitate, but then jettisoning all the complicated parts until you were left with one or two strokes. Thus the Chinese 加 (*ka*) was reduced to 力 to write the syllable *ka*.

When this process was complete, it resulted in the existence of a syllabary that today contains 48 basic symbols. These are called *katakana*. They are still used in modern Japanese, chiefly to write foreign words or where special spelling out of a difficult form is needed.

But, in case things were not complicated enough, the process did not stop there. There also developed another form of syllabic writing in Japanese, this time slightly more cursive than

る垂を範り至に今妙絶辭父文るつ上を之し著を語物氏源てし籠參に寺山石け受を命の院門東上部式紫

Writing Systems

the *katakana*. This was called the *hiragana*. Its origins are perhaps to be found in some surviving inscriptions from the 9th century AD. We know that the famous *Genji monogatari* (The Tale of Genji), which dates from the 11th century, was written entirely in *hiragana*. It is interesting that this was the work of an aristocratic woman called Murasaki Shikibu. Tradition relates that this form of cursive writing was developed by female courtiers and used chiefly by women in preference to the *kanji* that were mostly used by men. But it would not be correct to say that men never used *hiragana*, nor that women ignored the *kanji*.

To appreciate the more cursive nature of the *hiragana*, you only have to look at the symbol for the syllable *chi* ち, beside its *katakana* equivalent チ or the *hiragana* syllable *to* と beside the *katakana* equivalent ト.

So modern Japanese is a mixed logographic and syllabographic script. Although it is possible to write any Japanese text entirely in script of one type or the other, the normal practice is to use *kanji* for content words such as nouns and verbs and *hiragana* and *katakana* for grammatical markers that are part of indigenous Japanese grammar and have nothing to do with Chinese.

For example, consider at what a translation of "the cat sleeps on the mat" might look like, below.

Japanese signage

The signs on railway platforms in Japan typically show the station name in kanji (Chinese characters) as well as *hiragana* (Japanese cursive syllabary), because not all Japanese speakers may know the *kanji*. There is a transliteration in Roman characters for foreign visitors who do not read any Japanese.

You can see what a complex mixture this is of isolated *kanji* (with *kun* pronunciation) for the noun and verb, *hiragana* for particles and *katakana* to spell the foreign word *mat*.

猫	は	マ	ッ	ト	で	眠	る
KANJI (*kun*)	HIRAGANA	KATAKANA	KATAKANA	KATAKANA	HIRAGANA	KANJI (*kun*)	HIRAGANA
neko	ha = wa	ma	t(su)	to	de	nemu	ru
neko	*wa*	*matto*			*de*	*nemuru*	
cat	SUBJ	mat			on	sleeps	

The cat sleeps on the mat

Runes and Ogham

A form of the word *rune* is found in several Germanic languages and means *secret*. This gives a clue as to why they were invented.

The Germanic-speaking peoples of northern Europe had no written culture to speak of before about the 2nd century AD. They did not lack for contact with people who used writing: there was a modified form of the Greek alphabet in southern Gaul and among the Helvetii (a group of Celtic peoples settled in parts of modern Switzerland), North Etruscan script among peoples of northern Italy and, at various points, the developed Roman alphabet. Speakers of Germanic languages did not adopt any of these, but instead invented for themselves a system called runes. It has affinities with various northern Etruscan scripts but is by no means a simple adaptation. Germanic peoples had a fierce sense of cultural difference and wanted to keep to themselves. They did not adopt Roman letters until the end of the 5th century AD, and even then not in a concerted manner; runes remained in use to some extent until the 14th century AD.

Runic script

Runes are alphabetic in the sense that consonants and vowels are separately represented; they do not form a syllabary or abugida. But they are also not like most other alphabets because the letters do not follow the established common order that derives from Phoenician *aleph*, *bet*, *gimel*, *daled* and was taken over into Greek *alpha*, *beta*, *gamma*, *delta* and Roman A, B, C/G, D.

The order of letters in the runic script was quite different, the first six letters being *f, u, Þ (=th), a, r, k*. For this reason, the alphabet is known as the *fuÞark* (or *futhark*), see left. All 24 letters (later 16) are found in what became this fixed canonical order on the Kylver Stone, which dates from around AD 400 and was found on the Swedish island of Gotland in 1903.

The philologist Walter William Skeat (1835–1912) conjectured that the *futhark* were arranged acrophonically, that is to say that their order is based on the first letters of the first few words of the Lord's Prayer in an early Germanic form: *fader unser Þu an radorum*. This is a charming idea, but it is beyond belief that this system was invented to encode a Christian message at a place and time when Christianity was not to be established for many centuries. Even more importantly, this explanation says nothing about the order of letters beyond the first five. (It does not matter that it

f	u	th	a	r	k
g	w	h	n	i	j
p	ï	z	s	t	b
e	m	l	ng	d	o

The inscription on this stone at Ekeby, north of Stockholm, reads: "Gunni had these runes carved in memory of himself while alive. Þorgautr, Fótr's heir, carved these runes." Most Scandinavian runestones date from the late Viking age (AD 800–1066).

date from AD 450–600. One peculiar feature of ogham is that its symbols were designed to be carved at the corners of stone columns, on to two perpendicular planes simultaneously. Four straight parallel lines mean S if they go to the right but C if they go to the left; both at the same time are E. This was never intended to be an easy read! When, much later, they were written on parchment, an upright line was needed in each symbol to represent the edge of the stone.

The letters of the ogham alphabet are formed of up to five notches, carved into the edges of a rock. This script was used from the 4th century AD for very short Irish or Pictish inscriptions on stone monuments.

does not explain the *k*, because the word *futhark* was not itself invented until the 19th century).

The earliest use of the runes was always on stone or some other hard surface – their use in manuscripts was much later. In a manuscript written in Canterbury in the late 11th century AD, a runic charm is found invoking the blessing of the god Thor to drive away an illness causing pus in the blood vessels. This occult, magical element of the runes became more significant with time, and today they are often seen as part of the recovery of a pagan past in Europe.

Ogham

The element of secrecy is apparent in another unusual form of inscriptional writing called ogham. It originated in Ireland, probably in the 4th century AD. The majority of texts come from Ireland and

Decipherment

Most of the languages and writing systems discussed in this book have had reliable traditions of transmission. We know about Latin because it never really did die out, but for some languages this is not the case.

Latin is sometimes called a "dead" language, but there was a continuous tradition of use by Church and State, even if the language was not learned from the cradle. Ancient Greek also never went underground: the Byzantine Empire and the Greek Orthodox Church preserved texts and their meanings. Ancient Egyptian however, ceased to be a living language in the 1st century AD.

The last-known inscription in Ancient Egyptian is dated to AD 394 and all understanding of it was soon lost, to be recovered slowly and painstakingly only in 19th-century Europe. Similarly, the various languages that were written in cuneiform script – Sumerian, Akkadian, Hittite, Ugaritic, Eblaite, Old Persian – could not be read until cuneiform was deciphered in the 19th century. The feat was considerable because cuneiform is not one single system. Wedge-shaped writing was used in completely different ways to record very different languages, and many signs had differing values at different times and places.

Deciphering Ancient Egyptian

The decipherment of Ancient Egyptian is a story that has been told too often and too well to need detailed repetition here. As with any code, it was a question of finding a way in. Just as various German and Japanese military ciphers used in the Second World War were not broken in one easy step, so the hieroglyphs did not yield straightforwardly to investigation. The key lay in finding the right point of attack, and an element

of luck was also needed. In this case, that came with the discovery in 1799 by Napoleonic troops of an inscribed piece of granite at the fortress of El Rashid (Rosetta) in Egypt.

The Rosetta Stone records a decree from 196 BC concerning King Ptolemy. He was part of a Greek dynasty, so it was natural enough for part of the inscription to be written in Ancient Greek. This language was well known, of course, so scholars could read it with ease. Two kinds of Egyptian writing are found on the stone: the formal lapidary hieroglyphic and a much more cursive demotic.

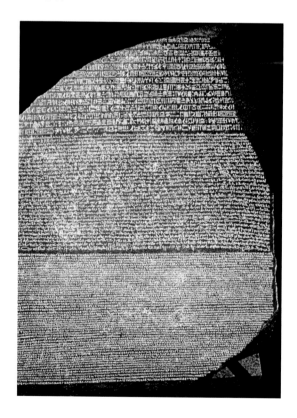

The text of the Rosetta Stone praises the deeds of King Ptolemy, from tax cuts to gifts to the temple, and describes plans for new statues in his honour.

Jean-François Champollion

By the age of 17, Jean-François Champollion had mastered six oriental languages, including Ethiopic and Arabic, and was working on a Coptic dictionary and grammar. From 1816 onward, he focused on deciphering Egyptian hieroglyphs. In 1822, he published his groundbreaking findings on the relationship between the different elements of the script, based on studying the Rosetta Stone.

It made sense to assume that they said the same thing as the Ancient Greek text.

The way in was found by Jean-François Champollion (1790–1832). He was not the first person correctly to decipher some Egyptian symbols – the British polymath Thomas Young (1773–1829) understood that some symbols represented sounds, but believed that these were limited to the writing of personal names marked by special oval borders called cartouches. He was prevented from getting any further because he thought that everything else written in hieroglyphs was purely ideographic.

Champollion took the step of supposing that values obtained for symbols used to write personal names could be applied elsewhere to read the rest of a text. Since he had a good knowledge of Coptic, which is the surviving descendant of Ancient Egyptian still used today for religious purposes among Christians in Egypt, he was able to make considerable progress in deciphering the script. His breakthrough was understanding that it is a mixture of phonetic elements and purely symbolic determinants (see Cuneiform and Hieroglyphs, page 134). This step taken, understanding of the Egyptian language accelerated considerably. It was not the work of a moment to unlock all the complexities of the writing and grammar, but all further work now rested on a secure basis.

Deciphering cuneiform

The decipherment of the many varieties of cuneiform came from one of its simpler deployments: the writing of Old Persian language. Once again, the key was a multilingual inscription carved into the face of an inaccessible cliff at Mount Behistun in northwestern Iran. It was done during the reign of Darius I (522–486 BC) and written in three different languages: Old Persian, Elamite and Babylonian.

The first serious copy of it was made in 1778 by a German mathematician and surveyor named Carsten Niebuhr. The decisive step in decipherment was made by Georg Grotefend (1775–1853), a brilliant German linguist who spotted that the cuneiform symbols used in writing Old Persian were being deployed more or less phonetically to write individual sounds (or syllables), whereas something else was going on in the other two texts.

The point of attack, as with the Rosetta Stone, was personal names. The names of the Persian kings known to the Greeks as Darius and Xerxes were tentatively identified by Grotefend. This allowed him to decipher more or less correctly about a third of the signs. Others with a better knowledge of Iranian languages, such as Rasmus Rask, Eugène Burnouf and Christian Lassen, took the work forward.

The British soldier, administrator and scholar Sir Henry Rawlinson (1810–95) had worked on Old Persian and went on to tackle the Babylonian texts. Although Rawlinson correctly conjectured that certain signs were personal royal names, they could not easily be read because it was clear that the writing was not alphabetic. But there are also in the Old Persian royal titles such as *great king* and *king of kings*. Once it was guessed

As with the Rosetta Stone, the names mentioned in the trilingual inscriptions on Mount Behistun in Iran helped lead to the decipherment of cuneiform.

that Babylonian was a Semitic language, the well-known related languages within the family could be used to decipher the word for *king*. The breakthrough came when it was realized that the script is a complex mixture of syllabograms and logograms (see Syllabic Writing, page 140). Here again, the system took time to yield up its subtleties but research was now on a sure footing. The Elamite portion of the text remains poorly understood because the language has no relatives.

Babylonian also provided the key to unlocking Sumerian. The two languages are quite unrelated and the scripts work quite differently, but there are some continuities in the representations of sound. Fortunately, Babylonian scribes left behind extensive glossaries explaining and sometimes giving the pronunciation of Sumerian words.

Deciphering Linear B

The great decipherment of the 20th century was that of Linear B, by the brilliant amateur Michael Ventris (1922–56). Although not a classical scholar, he had a logical mind and drew up grids charting sequences of signs that were the same except for their endings, so he conjectured that the language written by Linear B was inflected.

That finding had already been made by the brilliant American scholar Alice Kober (1906–50), whose so-called "triplets" had a similar function. She took Linear B words and arranged into groups of three those that had the same few symbols at the beginning. The second item had the same number of symbols but the last one was different. The third item always ended in a quite new and different character but was shorter by one character than the preceding two. Because there were so many instances of words where the beginning was the same but the endings were different, she concluded that Linear B was writing an inflected language where the endings change but the stem says the same. The triplets identified three kinds of ending.

Kober did not live long enough to understand the fuller significance of her findings; perhaps she would never have made the breakthrough. Ventris realized that these different endings probably indicated symbols for syllables that shared the same onset but a different rhyme, as you would get if you tried to spell out Latin *do-mi-nus, do-mi--ni, do-mi-no* using a syllabary. Kober's largely forgotten role in

the decipherment might be likened to that of Rosalind Franklin in the discovery of DNA.

There is always some decisive step and Ventris took it, guessing that some symbols in Linear B might have the same value as they did in the syllabic writing of Crete, which was understood. He then did what decipherers do, and looked for names. He found them. Once he had deciphered the writing for Amnisos, Knossos and Tylissos, he was able to feed those back into his grids and systematically unlock other names. This gradually led him to understand that he was dealing not with an alphabet, but a syllabary, and that the language written in Linear B was an early form of Greek. Many great scholars have worked on Linear B, including Anna Morpurgo Davies, who produced a lexicon of Mycenaean Greek in 1963.

The heyday of decipherment was probably the 19th century, following the new pathways opened by the Enlightenment. But the work continues today: although many languages have been deciphered, there are still outstanding tasks. Anyone who likes a challenge might like to take a look at the Indus Valley Script from Pakistan. After more than a century of work, decipherment has not been achieved and experts still disagree over basic questions.

Anna Morpurgo Davies

Born and educated in Italy, Anna Morpugo Davies (1937–2014) first studied Linear B as a classics student in Rome, not long after the language had been deciphered. She subsequently devoted her long and brilliant academic career to historical linguistics, specializing in Mycenaean and Anatolian philology.

Linguistic Variety

Linguistic variety is not neutral. People have attitudes about the kinds of speech that they find acceptable. Characters in books and films are often given habits of speech that are intended to mark them out as being different: the cold and sinister English aristocrat in an American film; or the characters in Aristophanes' plays whose broad vowel sounds mark them out as having come from other parts of Greece. These phenomena go beyond having a different accent; it is to do with variations in grammar and vocabulary.

The varieties of human speech are part of a fragile ecology. Countless local languages of Africa are eclipsed by Hausa, Swahili or Xhosa – the varieties connected with getting on in the world. Young people go to work in cities, the local language is no longer spoken at home and not taught to children. This happens throughout the world. You will look at what causes language death, and at efforts to slow it down.

Dialects

What separates a language from a dialect or an accent? The description of such differences is the business of linguists, but how people feel about them is a sociological issue.

Once, when I was a young undergraduate, I was back home at a party during the holidays. When it became known that I was studying languages at university, one of my fellow guests felt the need to grill me: "How many languages are there, then?" I said that it was hard to give even an approximate figure, but that it might be in the order of 7,000. "That many *languages*?" came the reply. "Surely not! Don't you mean *dialects*?"

I felt mildly put out that the questioner clearly thought I didn't know what I was talking about – but it was a fair question, all the same. To be able to count things means that it has to be possible to identify discrete entities. How can you do that with languages if you cannot tell where the boundaries between them fall?

Mutual intelligibility

An often-used rule of thumb is that two forms of speech are dialects of each other if there is mutual intelligibility between their speakers. French and Russian are separate languages: the ability to speak one does not confer understanding of the other. But what about Spanish and Italian? They are pronounced differently and have marked differences in spelling and grammar and

At the time of writing, in the order of 7,000 languages are spoken around the world.

Linguistic Variety

Italian

Una tazza di caffè, per favore

Spanish

Una taza de café, por favor

Italian speakers on holiday in Spain order a cup of coffee in their native language and still get what they want.

vocabulary, yet some speakers can understand some of what is spoken or written in the other language. Imagine an Italian in a Spanish café who asks the waiter for *una tazza di caffè, per favore* ("a cup of coffee, please"). The waiter might well understand, because in Spanish the equivalent is *una taza de café, por favor*. At that level, there is mutual understanding. But nobody could seriously argue that this holds at all levels. Imagine the Italian now asks *Cosa ti piace di più? I romanzi di Pavese o le commedie di Pirandello?* ("What do you like best? The novels of Pavese or the plays of Pirandello?"); it would not be so readily understood. The Spanish is *¿Qué te gusta más? ¿Las novelas de Pavese o las obras de Pirandello?* The two suddenly seem a long way apart in vocabulary and grammar.

The question often arises of just how much similarity there has to be before two varieties of speech are considered mutually intelligible. It might be tempting to say that, for example, 70 percent mutual intelligibility or more makes for two dialects, whereas 30 percent or less indicates separate languages. But who decides on the percentage? More importantly, what are we to count? The set of possible utterances is infinite and you cannot measure a percentage of infinity. If you choose just, say, 1,000 utterances, then you have largely predetermined the outcome.

Let us take some examples of terminological difficulty. The speech of Newcastle and that of Glasgow are somewhat different. People from those areas sometimes have trouble understanding each other's accents, and each variety has many

"There's an accent shift, on average, every 25 miles in England."

David Crystal

Speakers of Danish and Norwegian can, for the most part, understand each other, as can speakers of Hindi and Urdu. Italians speaking the local dialects of Venice and Sicily, however, can only understand each other up to a point, if at all, even though they are ostensibly speaking the same language.

words not commonly known by people outside the region. You might well talk about two dialects. On the other hand, the kinds of Italian spoken in Venice and Sicily are also called *dialetti*, but are far from mutually intelligible. Danish and Norwegian are usually presented as separate languages, yet their spoken varieties have a very high degree of mutual intelligibility. The same is true of Hindi and Urdu. The reason why mutually unintelligible varieties of Italian are called dialects, whereas Danish and Norwegian or Hindi and Urdu are called separate languages, must be sought in the realm of politics, not linguistics.

The problem with dialects

When a Spaniard goes on holiday to Venezuela, she will encounter a different variety of Spanish. But she does not need to go on a course to make herself understood; she just needs a passport and an aeroplane ticket.

It would be hard to describe Castilian and Latin American Spanish as two fundamentally different languages. But the term *dialect* is equally problematic because it suggests that there is a prestigious Castilian form of speech that is the

"language" of which the Venezuelan "dialect" is a non-standard, sub-standard or other deviant variety.

Linguists are acutely aware of this problem. It might be that people in, say, Paris hold views about the correctness or otherwise of the French spoken in Marseilles. They might also have opinions about the French spoken across Belgium or in Quebec. But these are cultural attitudes and more a matter of sociology than anything else. A linguist can describe the differences in pronunciation

It would be problematic to call the Spanish spoken in Venezuela a dialect of the Castilian spoken in Spain.

and spelling and grammar and vocabulary. But once you use a word like "dialect" to describe a particular form, you are attaching a label that has overtones that come from a different domain. For this reason, some linguists use the word *languoid* for any kind of speech that differs from another. This rather rebarbative term has not caught on, however, and most linguists have settled on the word "variety" instead. The idea is not that Swiss German is a variety of German, but that both are simply varieties; there is no normative form. People pretend that there is when they write textbooks for learners. Something has to be held up as usual – generally in the sense of how people talk on the news. But that is just a convenience, and does not do justice to the actual variations on the ground.

The linguist Max Weinreich (1894–1969) is dubiously credited with having said – in and about Yiddish – *a shprakh iz a dialekt mit an armey un flot* ("a language is a dialect with an army and a navy"). Whoever said it put a finger on the truth; much of what people say and how they feel about languages depends on the allegiances they feel to particular groups, regions or nation-states.

There are numerous differences between the varieties of German spoken in Switzerland and Germany, but one cannot be considered a dialect of the other.

Language Ecology and Death

The variety of human speech is generally taken for granted, or even seen as a nuisance, but many languages are at risk of dying out.

Early in 2010, the death was reported of Boa Sr. She was the last-known fluent speaker of Bo, a language spoken in the Andaman Islands in the Bay of Bengal. With her death a link was broken to an ancient culture and way of life. Nobody will tell stories in Bo any more. The waters have closed over whole areas of human memory and experience, as though all the generations of Bo speakers had never lived.

The phenomenon of language death is nothing new. Sumerian died out as a spoken language around 2000 BC. Egyptian died out as a vernacular in the 1st century AD. In those cases, however, not all is lost because large bodies of written material have survived and, thanks to heroic efforts in

decoding them (see Decipherment, page 156), can be securely read and understood. But with Bo and many of the other languages that are under threat today, this is not the case. Many, perhaps most, of these languages have no written culture and when they cease being spoken they will never be heard again. For those with the heart to notice, the silence will be deafening and deadening.

Why does language death matter?

For linguists, of course, language death is a sorry thing because languages are intrinsically fascinating. Their structures are interesting and they encode ways of looking at the world that are

The last-known fluent speaker of Bo, a language of the Andaman Islands in the Bay of Bengal, died in 2010.

When a language becomes extinct, we lose more than just vocabulary: a unique part of human culture and experience dies, and links with the past are irreparably broken.

at large. The loss of a language negates that. It is like the melting of another part of the polar ice-cap, or the deforestation of another part of the Andes, or the extinction of another endangered species.

This last comparison is perhaps the most apt. Languages are part of a fragile global ecology. Ecology is about diversity and we value diversity in and for itself. Languages go to the root of our identity; if you doubt this, just look at Ireland, Wales, the Languedoc in France, Catalonia, Serbia, Kashmir, Pakistan or any other zone where cultural identity is reflected in linguistic choices. It would be naive to imagine that strife would disappear if everyone spoke the same language. The history of the world is littered with counter-examples: the Russian revolution, the Rwandan genocide, the American Civil War are just three examples of deadly strife in monolingual territories. If everyone spoke English, it might be convenient for English-speaking businesses but a catastrophe for culture.

as varied as the cultures who use those languages. For humanity at large, though, it is nothing short of a cultural tragedy. The loss of individual humans is hard enough to bear, but some solace is usually taken in the thought of the survival of the culture

Parts of the French region of Pyrénées-Orientales are historically Catalan-speaking, and the Catalan flag is often displayed alongside the French Tricolour.

The island nation of Papua New Guinea is the most linguistically diverse place on Earth, with over 830 languages spoken. The nation's official languages are Tok Pisin, Hiri Motu and English, but the latter two are spoken by less than 2 percent of the population. Tok Pisin, an English-based Pacific pidgin that developed on plantations in the mid-19th century, is the most widely spoken and understood language.

And why do English speakers smugly imagine that they will be the winners in any process of globalization? What if, 75 years from now, they suddenly have to learn Chinese?

It has already been seen that language diversity is often greatest in countries where geographical and social factors have pulled against homogeneity. In Papua New Guinea, more than 830 languages are spoken in an area of 463,000 square kilometres (179,000 square miles) by about 8 million people. That is an unparalleled variety. The stark fact is that a quarter of the languages on Earth have fewer than 1,000 speakers, and of these languages it is estimated that perhaps half will be extinct in a century from now. That is a sickening prospect.

How do languages die?

Plainly, we can say that a language is dead when the last speaker dies. But that leaves an intermediate stage where it is hard to say what is happening. If there are only 10 speakers, we may assume that the language is on the verge of extinction. To have 100 speakers might be more encouraging, but the situation is still precarious;

about 500 languages are in this position. There is no minimum number of speakers that will, in all places, tell you whether a language can survive or not, but it would seem that having fewer than 500 speakers tends to be a marker for imminent trouble.

In 1991, the linguist Joshua Fishman (1926–2015) devised a scale known as the Graded Intergenerational Disruption Scale. It aims to capture with a numerical index the degree of health of a language. In a modified form published by linguists Paul Lewis and Gary Simons in 2010, it is called the Expanded Graded Intergenerational Disruption Scale (EGIDS) and runs from 0–10 (see opposite). The lower the number, the more viable the language. The worrying stages come in the second half: stage 6b represents a threatened language, a situation in which all generations can use it but only some of the child-bearing generation are transmitting it to their children. Stage 7 is where the fertile generation uses it but does not transmit it to children at all. At stage 8a the language is moribund and only grandparents and older people use it. Once things get to

LEVEL	LABEL	DESCRIPTION	UNESCO
0	International	The language is used internationally in business, education and a broad range of other activities.	Safe
1	National	The language has official or de facto recognition at the level of the nation-state, and is used for government, education, business and other communicative needs.	Safe
2	Regional	The language is officially recognized at the sub-national level for government, education, business and other functions.	Safe
3	Trade	The language is not officially recognized, but is used for business, social and other functions to transcend language differences across a region.	Safe
4	Educational	The language is in vigorous use, and literacy in the language is being transmitted through a system of public education.	Safe
5	Written	The language is used orally by all generations and is effectively used in written form in parts of the community.	Safe
6a	Vigorous	The language is used orally by all generations and is being learned by children as their first language.	Safe
6b	Threatened	The language is used orally by all generations but only being transmitted to the next generation by a portion of the child-bearing generation.	Vulnerable
7	Shifting	The child-bearing generation can use the language among themselves but are not transmitting it to their children.	Definitely endangered
8a	Moribund	The only remaining active speakers of the language are members of the grandparent generation.	Severely endangered
8b	Nearly extinct	The only remaining speakers of the language are elderly and have little opportunity to use it.	Critically endangered
9	Dormant	The language remains as a reminder of heritage identity for an ethnic community, but there are no proficient speakers.	Extinct
10	Extinct	No one retains a sense of ethnic identity associated with the language, even for symbolic purposes.	Extinct

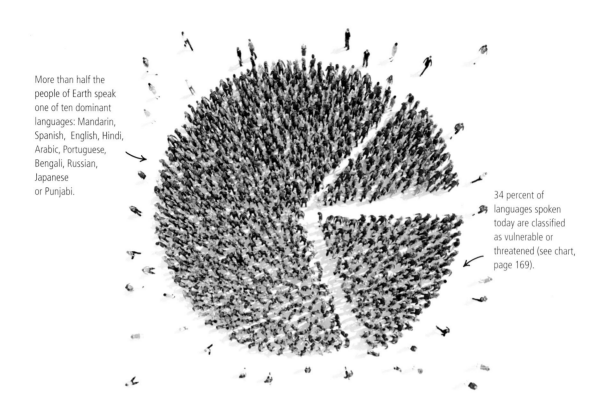

More than half the people of Earth speak one of ten dominant languages: Mandarin, Spanish, English, Hindi, Arabic, Portuguese, Bengali, Russian, Japanese or Punjabi.

34 percent of languages spoken today are classified as vulnerable or threatened (see chart, page 169).

this stage, the death of the language is almost inevitable unless effective steps are taken. The survival of a language as a living entity depends on cultural transmission; people have to teach it to their children and use it at home, if not at work.

Language death is an issue in all parts of the world. In Europe, for example, nearly 37 percent of the languages spoken are at stage 6b or below on the EGIDS scale, so they are at risk. In Africa, the figure rises to 45 percent. In continental Asia the figure is 38 percent and in the Pacific 34 percent. In the Americas, a staggering 61 percent of languages are threatened. The global figure for languages at or below stage 6b is 34 percent. At the other end of the scale, more than half the people on Earth speak one of ten dominant languages.

Action against language death

What can we do? The least that can be done is to record these languages against the eventuality that

Languages are at risk of dying out all over the world. Linguists undertake fieldwork to record native speakers before it is too late.

Linguistic Variety

In an effort to keep a threatened indigenous language alive, a road sign in British Columbia, Canada, shows place names in English and Squamish.

they do die out, which involves expensive fieldwork by trained linguists. Anthropologists started doing this in the US in the 1950s in an effort to record the dying languages of Native American groups. It meant making audio recordings where possible and also writing grammars and dictionaries so that these recordings could be understood by future investigators. Similar efforts are on foot all over the world: for the tribal languages of Africa, the indigenous languages of Australia and South America, and even the minority languages of Europe.

The real goal must be to bring some of these languages back from the brink. In Canada, funding has been found to revitalize Ojibwe, spoken chiefly in Quebec, Ontario and Manitoba. Although there are thousands of speakers, all varieties of the language are at or below stage 6b; now is the time to halt its decline. In France, similar work has gone into the promotion of Occitan (stage 6b) and Breton (stage 7). In the United Kingdom, Scots Gaelic is said to be at stage 2 because it is legally designated as a provincial language. But studies show that, in spite of widespread media and educational use, maintaining core users is still difficult. Welsh (also stage 2) is in a rather more vigorous state, at least in its traditional heartlands.

It is plain that it will not be possible to prevent the loss of many languages. But that does not mean that the game is not worth the candle, for real progress can be made. Cornish was once extinct but is reawakening (it was at stage 9 but is rising). The same is true of Squamish in British Columbia. The efforts being made are based on the conviction that language is not trivial: it goes to the heart of who we are.

What Next?

In this final part of the book, we shall be looking at invented languages and at the likely evolution of language in general. Perhaps the most famous invented languages are those created by J R R Tolkien for *The Lord of the Rings* in the mid-20th century. The growth in popularity of sci-fi and fantasy over the last half-century has seen the creation of far more imaginary languages, from Klingon to Dothraki. Books have been written on how to do it.

Natural languages change over time; pronunciation and vocabulary change, and even grammar evolves. Certain sounds get simplified, and some verbal forms (such as the subjunctive) are felt to be unnecessary. But increasingly, people are making proposals to alter language by deliberate intervention that we might call linguistic engineering, for example to eliminate features of the language that are felt to discriminate on the basis of sex. As the world becomes more self-conscious about language, we shall see more such interventions.

Artificial Languages

In ordinary language change, speakers' choices are sometimes unconscious and sometimes deliberate. With invented languages, however, we see a conscious act of creation. This is ironic because language was not originally created; it just happened.

The most famous and successful of invented languages, Esperanto is spoken by an estimated 2 million people around the world today.

Artificial languages fall into two types. The first is auxiliary languages, deliberately invented in the hope that people will adopt them as a second language. The best known of these is Esperanto, the creation of a Polish doctor called Ludwik Lejzer Zamenhof (1859–1917). In 1887, he published *Unua Libro* (First Book) under the pen-name Doktor Esperanto (which means in Esperanto "the doctor who hopes"). His goal was to make language learning simpler and to provide a means

of bringing people together across what he saw as the divisive boundaries of natural language.

The problem with auxiliary languages

There might be an element of blindness to human nature in this idea. A shared language is no guarantee of peace and goodwill – it did not save the English, Americans or Spaniards from bloody civil wars. Furthermore, language is more than a superficial means of labelling; it transmits culture and identity. It does this because it has a past; Esperanto, however, has practically none. That said, some 2 million people are estimated to speak it worldwide and perhaps a few thousands have learned it from birth. But then the current global population is a little more than 7.5 billion.

Esperanto is Indo-European in structure and vocabulary, so it will be particularly familiar if you speak a Romance language. It is hard to see what Esperanto has to offer in terms of internationalism if you are, for example, Russian or Chinese. You already have an old language that allows you to communicate with tens of millions of other people. If you are German and wish to talk to people in Nigeria, it is not clear why you would learn Esperanto rather than Hausa.

Esperanto might be the most famous and successful invented language, but it is not the only or the earliest one. Volapük was created around 1880 by a German priest named Johann Martin Schleyer (1831–1912), and it briefly had a fair number of enthusiasts. The problem was that its grammar was bafflingly complex and its spelling odd. Splits soon arose between factions with

different views about the way forward, and most adherents transferred their interest to Esperanto. It is now all but forgotten, even among linguists.

Ido and Interlingua are further attempts at the same goal. The topic could exhaust a whole book; not much would be gained by pursuing it here. People who are keen on internationalism are probably best advised to learn a natural language.

Conlangs

The second type of artificial language is the conlang or constructed language. These are invented as an exercise in fiction with no intention that they should be spoken in everyday life. When J R R Tolkien invented Quenya and Sindarin, for example, he did not offer them as alternatives to Esperanto. Rather, he was fleshing out Middle-

Volapük was too complicated to ever become the world language its creator Johann Martin Schleyer envisaged in his hymn to global communication.

earth, his mythological world, and the peoples in it. For him, as it happened, the linguistic impulse was primary – he thought of names and words and languages and then invented the peoples and history to go with it.

For Tolkien, Quenya was rather like Latin – the language of high culture and literature used by the High Elves. It has a complex system of noun inflection that actually makes it look rather like Finnish, which was a language that Tolkien particularly loved. The Low (or Grey) Elves were supposed to have spoken Sindarin, which bears much more likeness, in the formation of its plurals and the existence of consonantal mutation, to Celtic languages such as Welsh. This again is no accident, as Tolkien had a very great fondness for Welsh.

He did not stop at Elvish, though, and went on to create Dwarvish (or Khûzdûl) and even the Black Speech, the language of The Enemy and his servants, which he only worked out fragmentarily. But he also went to the trouble of designing an elaborate cursive script for Elvish and a runic alphabet for the dwarves, which befitted a race of workers in stone.

The impetus of Tolkien made itself felt in other areas. When *Star Wars* appeared in 1977, cinema-goers wondered at the guttural language of the Sand People and the high-pitched speech of the Jawas. The galaxy was obviously a place rich in languages – C3PO claimed to be fluent in more than 6 million forms of communication. But none of these was worked out in much detail.

In the world of *Star Trek*, the makers soon realized that Klingon and Vulcan would be interesting to explore. Klingon, in particular, has been elaborated over the decades, perhaps chiefly to please the fans. In *Star Trek VI: The Undiscovered Country*, Christopher Plummer played a Klingon warrior named General Chang, who proudly declared that one could not understand Shakespeare until one had read him in the original Klingon!

A Song of Ice and Fire (better known in its television incarnation, *Game of Thrones*) is arguably the fictional world that comes nearest to Tolkien's in terms of the depth of its history and complexity of cultures. George R R Martin himself did little in terms of conlangery beyond inventing names

J R R Tolkien

Perhaps the most famous invented languages are those created by J R R Tolkien for *The Lord of the Rings*. Tolkien was a professional philologist and an expert on Anglo-Saxon in particular, and knew what a language ought to sound and look like without really articulating the principles. Below are two lines from "Namárië", a poem Tolkien wrote in Quenya, the language of the Elves in his books, shown in Tengwar, an artifical script he invented, and in Latin script.

Ai laurië lantar lassi súrinen
Yéni únótimë vë rámar aldaron!

What Next?

"It's almost as if you can create an entire universe on your own."

David Peterson, Language Creator

and some words in his characters' languages. When the books came to television, the producers approached the American linguist and conlanger David Peterson, initially to create Dothraki and later High and Low Valyrian. A highly trained linguist with a deep understanding, he was well able to create languages that sound right to the ear and look plausible when written down. This is not a matter of luck, but of knowing the sorts of phonological principles described in Part II of this book. A conlang is much more acceptable if, at the deepest level, it has sounds and structures that are somehow related to what real human languages do.

In the television series *Game of Thrones*, the character Daenerys Targaryen addresses her dragons in High Valyrian and her horse-mounted warriors in Dothraki. Both languages were created by David Peterson.

The Future

Nobody can predict what any given language might be like in 100 or 500 years. But observing the past gives us some clues to the future.

Natural language change

Languages evolve naturally in use. New words are adopted all the time, some of which fall out of use after a while. French *à toute vapeur* ("full steam ahead") was common during the steam era; nowadays it is quaint. German *eitel* means *pure* (as in gold), but is nowadays scarcely used in that sense.

Morphology tends to be simplified. French, for example, has an imperfect subjunctive (*je donnasse*, *il donnât*), but the tendency for some decades has been to replace it with the present subjunctive, which is easier to form. I have heard people giggle when elderly professors use the older form. The minority who bother about the subjunctive in English will doubtless have disappeared within a generation or two.

Sounds alter as well, of course. Around 1950, English speakers in all regions pronounced *nephew* as if it were /neview/. Nowadays most people say /nefew/. The pace of such change is comparatively slow; there might be nothing to report in one person's lifetime. But in a century or so, changes will be noticed.

Deliberate language change

Spelling will definitely change. Sometimes this happens slowly, but sometimes a government decides to enact root-and-branch reform. The Russians did this with their alphabet after the Revolution. In France in 1990, far-reaching changes were adopted that actually affect grammar rules taught in school. Before then, the future of *céder* (*to yield*) was *je céderai*, with an acute accent. It is now *je cèderai* to make it match the present tense. As recently as 1996, German-speaking countries

The German *Eszett* can be replaced with *ss* if the character *ß* is unavailable. Until recently, it only existed as a lower-case letter, but in 2017, a capital "sharp s" was officially introduced.

did something similar, not least by altering the fiddly rules for the so-called *Eszett* or *scharfes S* (ß).

In time, there will be more deliberate interventions, but those who innovate have to walk the tightrope between making things simpler in the present and maintaining links with the past. Changing the rules makes it harder to understand things from before the reform.

But some changes seem overdue, for example in the area of gender. Many people are increasingly irritated by the fact that, in English, there are no gender-neutral pronouns or possessive adjectives; the default position is always masculine. Thus "the reader may doze if *he* will" or "the writer must take up *his* pen". If you want to highlight the problem, you might say "the writer must take up *her* pen". Many people are using the plural pronoun *their* in all such cases. This is not generally

Pronounciations shift over time: today's speakers of English do not say *nephew* in the same way people did in the 1950s.

felt to be grammatically correct at present, but socially it might be thought desirable to adopt it. Even some men are beginning, as they say, to check their privilege.

The situation is harder in languages like French, where every noun, animate or not, must have a grammatical gender that is masculine or feminine. But the default position is still usually masculine. Some changes have occurred: in the teeth of some resistance, a female *docteur* is now called *docteure*. A female ambassador is now an *ambassadrice*. In the past, when nobody could imagine a woman ambassador, the word could only mean *ambassador's wife*.

Changes in writing

What about writing? Many people abbreviate their spelling in SMS messages. Will this spread to newspapers? The popularity of emojis is surprising: people are turning the clock back 5,000 years and using pictographs like the ancient Egyptians. The problem is that the recipient does not necessarily understand the message to mean what the

sender intended it to. Of the many emojis that are supposed to denote a smile, for example, one looks to some people alarmingly like a grimace and so risks sending precisely the opposite message. Perhaps we are moving closer to the world of Humpty Dumpty in Lewis Carroll's *Through the Looking-Glass*, who used words to mean whatever he meant them to.

From abbreviations to emoji, mobile devices are changing the way we communicate in writing.

Glossary

For context-specific examples of the terms listed below, please refer to the Index.

Ablaut
Variation in *vowel* to alter the grammatical function of a word, as in the Greek *leipo, loipos, elipon* (e, o, nothing).

Abugida
A writing system made up of *syllabograms* resembling each other if they share the same *onset* but slightly modified to mark difference in *rhyme*. Also known as an alphasyllabary. Contrast *syllabary*.

Affix
An umbrella term for changes to the beginning, middle or end of a word.

Affricate
A *consonant* sound made up of a *stop* combined with a *fricative*.

Agglutinative, -nation
A language in which words are composed of *morphemes,* each of which has only one meaning.

Allomorph
A contextually determined variant of a single *morpheme*. For example, German *-t* (as in *gekauft*, meaning *bought*) and *-en* (as in *gewesen,* meaning *been*) are allomorphs of the past participle suffix.

Allophone
A contextually determined variant of a single *phoneme*. For example, English /pʰ/ in the word *pin* as opposed to /p/ in *spin*.

Alphabet
A writing system in which *vowels* and *consonants* are represented by separate symbols.

Alveolar
A *place of articulation* where the tongue is brought close to, or into contact with, the hard ridge behind the teeth.

Articulatory system
The vocal apparatus (such as the tongue, teeth, roof of mouth, *pharynx*) used in making sounds.

Aspect
A way of indicating whether the action of a *verb* is bounded in time or ongoing.

Aspirate, -ion
A *manner of articulation* in which a *stop* is accompanied by a puff of breath.

Back vowel
A *vowel* made with the highest part of the tongue toward the back of the mouth, such as U and O.

Bilabial
A *place of articulation* where a *stop* is made by bringing the lips close or fully together.

Bound morpheme
A *morpheme* that cannot stand by itself, such as *-tion, -ology, -ist, -er, -ed*.

C, C$_1$, C$_2$
Abbreviation for *consonant* or, where necessary, the first and subsequent *consonants* in a *syllable*.

Cardinal vowels
A series of eight *vowels* relative to which the location of other *vowels* may be described.

Close vowel
A *vowel* made with the tongue close to the roof of the mouth, for example, *i* as in *machine* or *u* as in *pool*. Contrast *open vowel*.

Closed syllable
A *syllable* of the shape $(C_1)VC_2$.

Cluster
A sequence of at least C_1C_2 but with more Cs possible.

Coda
Whatever, if anything, follows the *nucleus* of a *syllable*.

Consonant
Any sound that is not a *vowel* and thus involves some turbulence, constriction or obstruction in the airstream.

Dental
A *place of articulation* where the lips or tongue are brought close to, or into contact with, the teeth.

Ergativity, -ive
Where a *noun* that is the *subject* of an intransitive *verb* is marked the same as the object of a *transitive verb*.

Free morpheme
A *morpheme* that can stand by itself. For example, *bookkeeper* can be analysed into two free morphemes, *book* and *keeper*, the latter of which is itself one free morpheme (*keep*) and a bound agential suffix morpheme (*-er*).

Fricative
A *manner of articulation* in which air passing between *articulators* is constricted but not fully obstructed.

Fusional
Another word for *inflecting*.

Ideogram
A symbol used in a writing system to denote an abstract idea rather than a concrete thing. Numerals are ideograms, not being tied to individual languages. Contrast *logogram*, *pictogram*.

Infix A type of *affix* added within a word. If X is added to (e.g.) *CVC* to produce *CVXC*, then X is an infix.

Inflecting, -ection
A language that chiefly marks grammatical modifications to words by *affixing morphemes* that generally have more than one function. Contrast *agglutinative*.

Isolating
A monosyllabic language in which the ratio of *morphemes* to words is 1:1.

Labiodental
A *place of articulation* where the lower teeth are brought close to, or into contact with, the upper lip.

Lexeme
The fundamental form of a word, irrespective of *affixes* or *ablaut*. For example, *take* is the fundamental form of which *taken* or *took* are modifications

Lexicon
The sum total of *lexemes* in a language.

Logogram
A symbol used in a writing system to denote a spoken word. Contrast *ideogram, pictogram*.

Manner of articulation
Other features present in the articulation of a *consonant* once the *place of articulation* is fixed.

Minimal pairs
A pair of words in a given language that differ in meaning because of a difference in a single *phoneme*, for example French *pain* (bread) and *bain* (bath).

Morpheme
The smallest unit of meaning: may be a word or part of a word. For example, *un-* in *undone; keeper* is *keep* and *-er* (one morpheme is *free*, the other *bound*).

Nasal
A sound whose articulation is accompanied by the lowering of the soft palate, as in French *bon* (good).

Noun
A word that names a person or a concrete or abstract thing.

Nucleus
The part of a *syllable* between the *onset*, if any, and the *coda*, if any.

O
Abbreviation for object, the person or thing to whom the action of a *verb* is done.

Onset
Whatever comes before the *nucleus* of a *syllable*.

Open syllable
A *syllable* of the shape *V* or *CV*.

Open vowel
A *vowel* made with the tongue low in the mouth. Contrast *close vowel*. For example, *bat* is open; *beat* is close. Both are *front*.

Palatal
A *place of articulation* where the tongue is brought close to, or into contact with, the hard palate.

Pharyngeal
A *place of articulation* where the root of the tongue is brought close to, or into contact with, the back of the *pharynx*.

Pharynx
Part of throat farther back than the mouth and farther forward than the voice box.

Phone
A single speech sound.

Phoneme
A *phone* whose replacement by a different one would alter the meaning of a word, for example as in *pin* and *bin*.

Phonotactic rules
The principles governing what sequences of *vowels* and/or *consonants* are found in a given language.

Pictogram
A symbol in a writing system that denotes an object by simply drawing it.

Place of articulation
Describes where in the mouth the *articulators* come closest together in making a *consonant*.

Prefix
A type of *affix* added to the beginning of a word. If X is put before (e.g.) *CVC* to produce X*CVC*, then X is a prefix.

Rhyme
The *nucleus* and *coda* of a *syllable*.

Rounded vowel
A *vowel* made with rounding of the lips, such as the *u* sound in *pool*.

S
Abbreviation for *subject*.

Sonority
The inherent loudness of a sound: some carry more than others.

Stop
A *manner of articulation* in which a *consonant* is produced by bringing two *articulators* fully together.

Subject
Describes the person or thing who performs the action of a *verb*.

Suffix
A type of *affix* added to the end of a word. If X is put after (e.g.) *CVC* to produce *CVC*X, then X is a suffix.

Syllabary
A writing system in which each symbol indicates a *syllable* and each differs from the others irrespective of whether the *syllables* written share *onset* or *rhyme*.

Syllable
A sound that can stand alone or with others to make a word. In the latter case, the component units are called syllables. A syllable may be further analysed as follows: the minimal shape of a syllable is *V*. Beyond that, what is possible depends on the *phonotactic rules* of the given language. Some possible shapes are *VC, VCC, CV, CVC, CCVC, CCVCC*.

Syllabogram
In a writing system, a symbol that stands for a *syllable*. Compare *logogram*.

Synthetic
An umbrella term to describe *agglutinating* and *inflecting* languages as opposed to *isolating* ones.

Tense
A way of indicating when the action of a *verb* took place in relation to a given timeframe.

Tonality
A feature whereby the voice can go up, down, up and down, or remain level with the *rhyme* of a single *syllable*.

Transitive
Used of a *verb* that necessarily requires an *object*.

Trill
A *manner of articulation* in which one *articulator* is brought close to another so that audible vibration results.

Unaspirated
A *stop* that is not *aspirated*, such as the *p* in *spin*.

Unrounded vowel
A *vowel* produced with the lips either spread or in a neutral position, such as the /a/ in *back*.

V
Abbreviation for *vowel*.

Velar
A *place of articulation* where the back of the tongue is brought close to, or into contact with, the soft palate.

Verb
A word that indicates an action or process.

Voice, -d, -ing (1)
A feature of sound made when the vocal cords are vibrating. All *vowels* are voiced by nature, whereas *consonants* need not be.

Voice (2)
A *verb* in the active voice indicates that the *subject* is performing the action. If it is in the passive, the subject is on the receiving end of the action of the *verb*. A *verb* in the middle voice indicates that the *subject* is performing the action for or to him/her/itself.

Vowel
A sound produced when air passes through the vibrating vocal cords without turbulence, constriction or obstruction in the airflow.

Bibliography

Evolutionary Aspects
M Tallerman and K R Gibson (2012), *The Oxford Handbook of Language Evolution* (Oxford: Oxford University Press)

General Linguistics
J Aitchison (2010), *Aitchison's Linguistics* (London: Hodder Education)
This book has very helpful suggestions for further reading.

P H Matthews (2014), *Oxford Concise Dictionary of Linguistics*, 3rd edition (Oxford: Oxford University Press)
A great resource for quick definitions with helpful examples.

Invented Languages
D J Peterson (2015), *The Art of Language Invention* (New York: Penguin)
A very readable modern survey by a well-trained linguist.

J Allan (1978), *An Introduction to Elvish* (Hayes: Barn's Head Books)
A classic repository of material on the languages of J R R Tolkien.

Language Death
D Crystal (2000), *Language Death* (Cambridge: Cambridge University Press)
A good outline of the problem of language death and what might be done.

D Nettle and S Romaine (2000), *Vanishing Voices: The Extinction of the World's Languages* (Oxford: Oxford University Press)
An excellent treatment of the topic.

Language Diversity
D Nettle (1999), *Language Diversity* (Oxford: Oxford University Press)
This book has a wealth of maps and statistics and explains why linguistic diversity is higher in some parts of the world than others.

Lexicon
G Deutscher (2011), *Through the Language Glass: Why the World Looks Different in Other Languages* (London: Arrow)
An excellent study of what you can and cannot deduce from vocabulary.

D Bellos (2012), *Is That a Fish in Your Ear: Translation and the Meaning of Everything* (London: Penguin)
Another excellent guide to sensible thinking about linguistic difference.

Morphology
G Deutscher (2005), *The Unfolding of Language* (London: Heinemann)
Excellent in particular on historical aspects.

P H Matthews (2009), *Morphology*, 2nd edition (Cambridge: Cambridge University Press)
This books gives a more detailed academic treatment.

Phonetics & Phonology

International Phonetic Association (1999), *Handbook of the International Phonetic Association* (Cambridge: Cambridge University Press)
This book is indispensable.

B Collins and I M Mees (2013), *Practical Phonetics and Phonology*, 3rd edition (London: Routledge)
Has a CD with useful audio.

P Ladefoged and I Maddieson (1996), *The Sounds of the World's Languages* (Oxford: Blackwell)
An excellent tour of the less-known sounds

Syntax

F Palmer (1983), *Grammar*, 2nd edition (London: Penguin and English Language Book Society)
This book is old but very readable.

World Languages

Asya Pereltsvaig (2017), *Languages of the World*, 2nd edition (Cambridge: Cambridge University Press)
An excellent region-by-region survey.

Anatole V Lyovin, B Kessler and W R Leben (2017), *An Introduction to the Languages of the World*, 2nd edition (Oxford: Oxford University Press)
Along similar lines as the title above, but with more detailed grammatical studies of selected languages.

Writing

P T Daniels and W Bright (1996), *The World's Writing Systems* (Oxford: Oxford University Press)
The ultimate resource on the subject.

Index

Index

Author's Acknowledgements

Without the continued love and support of my wife, Jane Beverley, this book could never have been started or finished. I am also very grateful to Stephen Colvin (*sine quo non*), Patrick Stiles, Paolo Vaciago and Mark Weeden. Needless to say, they are not responsible for my final views.

Publisher's Acknowledgements

With thanks to Ella McLean for additional typographical illustrations and Alice Ball at IllustrationWeb.

Picture Credits

123RF Jose Ignacio Soto 138; Łukasz Stefański 98; aniwhite 6; Beatriz Gascn 29b; Bohdana Bergmannova 71l & r; Dusan Loncar 132br; Ewelina Kowalska 16l; Katarzyna Katarzyna Białasiewicz 46; liligraphie 38; Mikhail Mischchenko 127; Richard Koizumi 149b; rihardzz 74; Roman Fedin 69b; Roman Fedin 170a; Uldis Zile 7b; Vladislava Ezhova 30; Vyacheslav Biryukov 43l; **Alamy Stock Photo** Art Collection 151a; Art Collection 2 131b; Arterra Picture Library 157l; Atomic 155a; Barry Vincent 111; Chronicle 68; dpa picture alliance 178; Everett Collection 122, 176; FalkensteinFoto 55, 67; Granger Historical Picture Archive 84, 145; ImageBroker 69a; Interfoto 83; Konrad Wothe/LOOK Die Bildagentur der Fotografen GmbH 166; Lebrecht Art and Music 152; Michele and Tom Grimm 170b; North Wind Picture Archives 133; Panther Media 148; Reynold Sumayku 15b; The Print Collector 107b; UtCon Collection 175; World History Archive 141; Xinhua 149a; **Bridgeman Images** Ashmolean Museum, University of Oxford 130 right; De Agostini Picture Library/Biblioteca Ambrosiana 108b; Pictures from History 114, 146; **Dreamstime. com** Alantunnicliffe 35; Alexander Kovalenko 36l; Alexzel 81; Almoond 162; Antartis 168r; Anton Eine 103a; Bravissimos 165; Byelikova 109 l & r; Deniscristo 132l; Elenabsl 40; Ferdinand Reus 58; Hanhanpeggy 12a; James Wagstaff 167; Jdanne 174; K45025 143; Katarepsius 154; Korkwellum 14; Kotist 126a; Lnmstuff 150a; Lukaves 17; Maksym Yemelyanov 48b; Marcio Goldzweig 126b; Michal Knitl 168l; Mogens Trolle 108a; Olga Lebedeva 132ar; Robot100 167a; Ruletkka 164; Sabuhi Novruzov 126c; Sergey Lavrentev 45; Shannon Matteson 150b; Snapgalleria 119; Steve Byland 11b; Suse Schulz 130l; Syda Productions 151b; Thirdrome 137; Tsung-lin Wu 10; Vectordraw 36r; Vladimir Timofeev 140; Welcomia 57; Ylivdesign 116; **Getty Images** Berk Ozkan/Anadolu Agency 93; Hulton-Deutsch Collection/Corbis 124; Leemage 157r; Library of Congress/VCG via Getty Images 120; Universal History Archive 156; Vivienne Sharp/Heritage Images 158; Werner Forman/Universal Images 112; Yves Gellie/Gamma-Rapho via Getty Images 63; **Metropolitan Museum of Art** Purchase, Raymond and Beverly Sackler Gift; 1988/public domain/1.0 134; **National Portrait Gallery, London** Photographs Collection 88; **Octopus Publishing Group** 290Sean@KJA Artists 16r; with permission of the President and Fellows of **Queens' College; Cambridge** 101; **REX Shutterstock** AP 49; **Shutterstock** Fedor Selivanov 135; Apple_Express_Japan 153; pikcha 179; **Wellcome Images** 86; 94; © Warner Brothers 24; **Wikimedia Commons** 61a; Bpilgrim/CC BY 2.5 95; British Library Harley MS 6325 61b; CC BY 2.0/Doods Dumaguing/Flickr 47; CC by SA 3.0/from Daniel Jones: An Outline of English Phonetics, W Heffer & Sons, 1972 25r; CC By SA 3.0/Walters Art Museum. Acquired by Henry Walters; 1927 31; Natalie Moxam 171; Östasiatiska Museet 113; Schoyen Collection 96.

Illustration Credits

Bill Hope at illustrationweb.com
cover illustration, 7, 12, 21, 22, 23 bottom, 26, 28, 32, 34, 39, 43 right, 44, 51, 59, 66, 75, 80, 85, 89, 91, 97, 103, 107, 115, 117, 118, 121, 127, 138, 144, 147, 155, 159, 163, 177, 179

Peter Liddiard at suddenimpactmedia.co.uk
11, 13, 15, 20, 23 top, 27, 33, 41, 50, 62, 79, 87, 98, 100, 105, 110, 117, 137

Editorial Director *Trevor Davies*
Senior Editor *Alex Stetter*
Copy Editor *Laura Gladwin*
Designer *Tracy Killick*
Illustrators *Bill Hope at Illustrationweb.com and Peter Liddiard at suddenimpactmedia.co.uk*
Picture Researchers *Giulia Hetherington, Jennifer Veall*
Production Controller *Grace O'Byrne*